FOOTBALL
THE EARLY YEARS

THE FOOTBALL BOOK WRITTEN BY A FAN
FOR ALL FOOTBALL FANS

FIRST PUBLISHED IN GREAT BRITAIN BY
SIMON MYERS, 'PALM BANK', 43 ELMLEY CLOSE,
OFFERTON, STOCKPORT, CHESHIRE SK2 5XE

© SIMON MYERS 2008

ISBN: 978-0-9560067-0-7

Printed & bound by
Fine Print (Stockport) Ltd.
Unit 6F, Lowick Close
Newby Road Industrial Estate
Hazel Grove, Stockport
Cheshire SK7 5ED
Tel: 0161 484 2244
www.fineprint-stockport.co.uk

Introduction

Football is a game that is now so closely bound up with the life of a nation. Hundreds and thousands of men and women play it, millions of both sexes watch it, every week during the season. To the great majority of these people, football is the main interest of life!

There have been many books published on the subject of Britain's most popular sport - Association Football. To the best of my knowledge, **there has never been one which contains as many facts** about the early history of the game as this one.

Some books in the past have covered different parts of football and moved around from one period to another. For easy reading, I have featured all the interesting **events in chronological order.** All the **origins of the sport,** outside and inside England have been included, along with Acts of Parliament banning football, the problems of the game being played in cities and towns and the importance of the Public Schools and Universities.

I have included details of **how every Football League Club started - each fan can see exactly how their club fits into football history.** To ensure accuracy, the information is based on details originally supplied by the Club Secretaries - written within living memory of the actual events. It is quite possible that some of the facts are unknown, even to the clubs themselves!

This is one of the few books which covers the **world's first ever football club, Sheffield F.C.** and the **Sheffield Association,** outlining their importance in the development of the game in the early years.

The **world's oldest football ground** is featured, the sport having been played there since 1860 and still used today!

Also included, is the story of how **the Football Association was formed 145 years ago,** back in 1863, and the problems it had in trying to co-ordinate all the different rules of football, as well as dealing with a lack of money to govern.

The **introduction of the F.A. Cup** in 1871 is discussed - the first Cup Final crowd of less than 2,000 witnessing the game at the Oval Cricket Ground! The winning goal was scored by a player who turned out illegally!

Whilst it is now taken for granted that players are **paid for playing football,** back in the 1880s, it was one of the **most controversial subjects to hit the game.** Read about the methods many clubs used, to try to 'hide' payments to their team! **Preston North End was expelled from the F.A. Cup** for this infringement!

The clubs from the industrial north soon took over from the Amateur teams from the south. Read the story of how a small Cheshire village team reached the last 16 of the F.A. Cup competition in 1886, how a **non-League club won the Cup** and how, on another occasion, the **Cup was taken out of England!**

All the changes in football rules appear in chronological order, including some old methods of actually marking the pitch! The **first overseas tour** by a football club in 1873, the **start of International matches** and the **first match to be played under floodlights in 1878** are included.

Also featured are the **venues for Cup Finals** - the Oval, Fallowfield, Crystal Palace, Old Trafford and Stamford Bridge, before Wembley in 1923.

William McGregor, a committee member of Aston Villa **established the Football League in 1888** - with just 12 clubs playing 22 games each.

The **first tables of the major Leagues are shown** - some of the clubs only of local interest now.

You will have heard of Test Matches at cricket, but did you know there used to be **Test Matches** also **at football?**

Last, and by no means least, it is important that any football book should include a **good selection of photographs.** I have searched the country archives to put together, some of the **oldest and most important pictures** ever assembled in one publication.

The history of football has been a long and fascinating story. I hope you enjoy the journey!

17th Century Italian Calcio in Florence - at least the pitch was the correct shape!

FOOTBALL : The Early Years

Historians are not able to tell us exactly when and by whom football was first played - it is one of the several sports that grew from a ball game. At Chester a victory over the Danes was celebrated by a game of football - the 'ball' being the head of a fallen enemy!

Many fans may think the game started not long before the FA Cup and the Football League, but by that time it already had many centuries behind it, perhaps a thousand years of history. In considering its long story, many people ask questions - who invented it? Where did it come from?

Whether for example football originated as pagan ritual - a combat or symbolic war between communities, certainly when it first appears in written records, it is as a game, if a very violent and undisciplined one!

How little does the world know what it owes the great schools and universities for the part they played in bringing some sort of shape and order to football.

It has often been stated that the Romans brought the game (like many other things) as conquerors to Britain, but the start can be traced much further back than that. The researches of a Professor H.A. Giles of Cambridge University show that a form of football existed at a far earlier date. The evidence he has unearthed points to China as the true origin in the third and fourth centuries B.C. when the game formed a part of the military training of that period. There is support for this in a military textbook of twenty-five chapters, dating from the Han dynasty some 2,000 years ago. Within, it included the expression 'Tsu Chu' which translated: TSU 'to kick the ball with the feet' - CHU the ball, made of leather and stuffed.

Here can be detected two basic differences in the game. In one form of it, two long bamboo poles, over thirty feet in height were set up, decorated with brightly-coloured silks in front of the Royal Palace on the Emperor's birthday. A silk net was stretched between poles with an opening of one foot in diameter - this was a game of shooting at goal, each player taking turns to

3

put the ball through the small opening. There were all the rewards and punishments for the contestants - the winners received fruits and wine and flowers and silver bowls, but the captain of the losing side was flogged!

The alternate pattern of this early Chinese game described the proficient player as one who uses the back, shoulders, breast and belly to take the place of feet; one who can withstand several opponents, making the ball run around his body without dropping as opposed to the 'shooting in' - here was clearly a form of early 'dribbling'.

As further evidence, around 1950 a Chinese team visited the U.K. from Hong Kong. They told of details available at home showing the first humble steps of the game, museum pieces such as beautifully ornamented goalposts which emperors used to give each other to mark festivals and birthdays. There were also ball games in Kyoto, Japan and Mexico where the ball represented the sun, the punishment for the defeated men in Mexico was even more drastic than China - they were sacrificed!

Before turning our attention back to our own island, we need to mention one more interesting fact in the form of football. Focusing on the picturesque and medieval Florence, the game of Calcio played in the Piazza Della Signoria twice a year - staged in May and June as public holidays. The opposing sides in white and red - twenty-one per side - face each other across the Piazza covered in sand, the whole width of the arena at each end forming the goals.

This game has been linked with the Roman sport of Harpastum, although the Italian one used a large ball and the Roman version a small one. However, they were team games played on a rectangular field with a centre-line and two base-lines; and the object was to throw the ball so that it eventually dropped behind the enemy's base-line. The ball was passed from player to player, it could be taken first bounce, but was dead if it bounced twice. Some form of tackling was permitted and descriptions have analysed the basic functions of Rugby football. This is the game which has been regarded as the starting point of football. It was popular in the ancient world, both Greek and Roman, for at least 800 years, and must surely have been played in this country by Roman soldiers and perhaps passed on to Romanised Britons. It was not really like primitive football, but much more highly developed and sophisticated.

The Romans had other ball games, requiring different types of balls - it is possible that one or other of these is the beginning of football.

The claims of the Angles, Saxons and others, whose invasions filled the period between the decay of Roman power and the coming of the Normans, must be considered. These were the people who in the end became the English nation and one might expect that a popular sport would find its origin with them.

The geographical distribution of football in later centuries does suggest that it belonged to the Anglo-Saxon's - there is a link between the areas where the game in various forms was later played and the territories of the early Anglo-Saxon kingdoms.

In at least two places, the local Shrovetide or other festival football was thought to be of a Saxon origin. Tradition says that there was football in Derby in A.D. 217 - in that year the men of Derby are supposed to have driven out of town a body of Roman soldiers and to have celebrated the event by a football carnival, which thereafter was played annually on Shrove Tuesday. Later these games ceased to be football and became unscrupulous group fights between the men belonging to the parishes of St. Peter's and All Saints, the point debated being the boundaries of the respective parishes. The last Derby game was played in 1846 - the term 'Derby Game' is still used today.

Some interesting superstitions connect football with the fertility of the crops - at Whitby it was believed that any young man who was ineffective at the game on Shrove Tuesday would be equally ineffective the following harvest! There were other football practices in connection with fertility - it was not uncommon for the opposing sides to consist of married men and bachelors respectively. Later in Chester, all men married within that year had to provide a symbolic silken ball.

There are many other Shrovetide customs and rituals - cock-fighting and cock throwing, hen-threshing, bell-ringing, the eating of pancakes and dumplings! There were many Shrovetide games as well - hockey and shuttle-cock at Leicester, trap-ball at Bury St. Edmunds and archery at Chester.

The first recorded history of English football begins with an account by a William Fitzstephen of Shrovetide festivities written in 1175. This document gives a clear picture of Norman London, and among other amusements , includes a game of ball which has been identified as football. We are told how the morning of Shrove Tuesday is spent cock-fighting and other boyish sports. Then:

> 'after dinner all the youth of the city proceed
> to a level piece of ground just outside the city
> (probably Smithfield) for the famous game

of ball. The students of every different branch have their own ball: and those who practise the different trades of the city theirs too. The older men, the fathers and the men of property, come on horseback to watch the contest of their juniors and in their own way share the sport of the young men; and these elders seem to have aroused in them a natural excitement at seeing so much vigorous exercise and participating in the pleasures of unrestrained youth.'

At the end of the 13th century there is a record of a fatality during a game at Ulgham (Northumberland) - we are told there were many players, and the accident arose when two men wearing daggers collided violently!

Football had not yet begun to be a nuisance in London: there were more open spaces and fewer narrow lanes than in the later city, hence less chance of footballers annoying shopkeepers and householders or provoking the authorities to take action against them. It was also played in other towns across most of the country.

For centuries, long before cricket was established, the people loved the rush and struggle of the crude and manly game of football. Without question, it is the oldest of all English national games - youth of London played in the surrounding fields and later in Covent Garden, Fleet Street and the Strand - hard to believe now!

With the 14th and 15th centuries a clearer picture of what part football played in English life appears - during this period for the first time it is one of our principal national sports and also for the first time as a forbidden sport! There were two main reasons for the ban - in the first place the game had become a nuisance and a danger when played in the streets of London and secondly it was regarded as a rival to archery. A proclamation was issued in the name of the King, Edward II via the Lord Mayor of London in 1314 banning football under the threat of imprisonment!

Another death was recorded in 1303, 'Thomas of Salisbury, a student of Oxford University found his brother Adam dead - and it was alleged that he was killed by Irish students playing ball in the High Street towards Eastgate'. The Irish students at Oxford were notorious for their wildness - the intentions of stopping football was to reduce such incidents.

There were plenty of accidents of a less serious kind during the 14th century - there is a record of two broken legs incurred while playing the game after a christening and of an internal injury resulting from a kick. This is the only instance of a football injury cured by miraculous means - the victim one William Bartram of Caunton (Newark), having been kicked in a 'sensitive place' during the early part of the reign of Henry VII suffered long and endurable pain, but suddenly recovered when he had seen the glorious King Henry.

A very gruesome incident in 1321 was reported when two murderers, brothers named Oldyngton of Darnhall, Cheshire were found playing football with the head of their victim, a certain John de Boddeworth, servant of the abbot of the monastery of Vale Royal (Near Northwich - monastery long gone, now a Golf Club).

A succession of Kings banning football on the grounds that it interfered with archery suggests first that it must have become a very popular sport and secondly it must have been played all over the country by the kind of men who made the best archers - if Kings and governments regarded it as a national danger in time of war, it must have been fast becoming a national game.

Outside London the local authorities seem at first to be reluctant to enforce the royal ban on sports - Henry IV in 1410 found it necessary to impose a fine of 20s. on mayors where football occurred. In 1450 at Halifax, an injunction was laid on persons playing football, dice or bowls under pain of penalty of 12 pence.

Despite all this anti-football legislation there is no evidence that the game became any less popular.

The period from Henry VIII to the start of the Commonwealth must have been a golden age for football. It becomes more and more popular as we approach the end of the 16th century. The game met with more opposition at that time than at any other and for the first time became a subject of controversy. Doubtless it was still a game for the city mob, but there is evidence that is was now sometimes played by all classes.

Shrove-tide football accompanied by traditional ceremony began to attract attention - in Chester violent contests in the streets had become a big problem.

Though football was so popular during this period, it was still illegal. Henry VIII (1509-47) was the last ruler to re-enact 'The bill for maintaining artillery and the debarring of unlawful games'. It must be assumed that after this time football and other games ceased to cause any interference with military training, but continued to come into collision with the law for other reasons.

We find local authorities in various places still banning football because it was a nuisance and led to disorder. In 1594 the council at Shrewsbury placed a ban on the game plus bear-baiting or bull-baiting within the town walls. No objection though for these sports taking place outside, likely to cause problems within the narrow streets of the town.

Moving to Manchester in 1608, the court records show for the first time the breaking of windows, though footballs must have been doing this on many previous occasions! A fine was the normal penalty for this offence, this incident being twelve pence.

A few years later in 1618, special football officers were appointed to deal with 'lewd and disordered persons', who chose to play football in the streets.

Very effective methods were adopted at Chester in 1533 and in the following years. Referring to Shrove Tuesday football in the city, the ball was presented by the Shoemakers' Company to the Drapers' Company before the game began - thanks to the participation of 'evil disposed persons', there had arisen 'great inconveniences'.

> ... 'Much harme was done some in the great
> thronge fallinge into a trance, some having
> their bodies bruised and crushed; some their
> arms, heades or leggs broken, and some
> otherwise maimed or in peril of their lives.'

Not unlike today's game! The Mayor was determined to put a stop to it - instead of banning it, he converted it to a better use, substituting a foot-race for the football match, the origin of the present Chester races for which the prize was a silver bell weighing two ounces.

Prosecutions for playing football were more frequent during this period, yet the records of them are quite outnumbered by other references to the game and there is no doubt that the law was more honoured.

At Worcester in 1633, a number of labourers were before the courts for just playing football - no doubt it often depended on the attitude of the local magistrates and there must have been many, who approved of football, who did very little to enforce the law.

During the 16th century a new attack started, more powerful because it was based on moral and religious grounds.

The Puritan attack on sport in general and Sunday sport in particular, found in football one of its chief targets. We have seen, during the Middle Ages, Sunday afternoon was devoted to amusement and pleasure, often centring in the church itself, and how football was played on Sundays.

In 1572 the Bishop of Rochester had demanded that Sunday football should be stopped - one Richard

Jeffercy in 1592 appeared before the Archdeacon of Essex on the charge that he 'had procured company together and plaied at foote-ball in Hackwell on Easter Monday in Evening Service time, and on pleading ignorance of the fact that a service was going on, was ordered to pay four pence to the poor'.

In the Middlesex County Records of 1613 another case of a man charged for organising rather than merely playing football - even spectators were sometimes prosecuted! In Bedford two men were in trouble for watching the game on a Sunday - one wonders how all the players managed to escape unidentified! Even more oddly, in 1616 at Guisborough (Yorkshire) when a man before the Special Sessions not for playing football or even watching but 'for making a banquett for football players on the Sabaorg'. Two men were fined 2s. for playing in St. Werburgh's cemetery at Chester during sermon time.

In 1618 James I issued his *Declaration of Sports* which expressly authorised the playing of games on Sunday and is therefore a direct counterblast to Puritan teaching. The prohibition of sport he complains,

> 'Barreth the common and meaner sort of
> people from using such exercises as may take
> their bodies more able for war, when we or
> our successors have occasion to use them.
> And in place thereof sets up filthy tipplings
> and drunkenness and breeds a number of
> idle and discontented speeches in their Ale-
> houses.'

Charles I re-issued the same declaration on the subject and took a much stronger view that sport should be played.

Some of a religious belief thought it divine judgment overtaking people in 1634 near Gainsborough on a Sunday, fourteen young men were playing football on the frozen river Trent when coming together in a scuffle, the ice broke and eight were drowned.

On the whole Sunday football was allowed to continue for the time being as long as Charles was in a position to assert his authority, yet in Hexham (Northumberland) in 1647 a fine of 2s. was fixed for playing football on the Sabbath.

In 1653, the first year of the Commonwealth, four men were summoned at Maidstone for playing the game plus several other people - the justices fined the Constables for not arresting them. In 1655 Manchester Court ordered the Constables to stop anyone playing within the streets of the town.

To judge from what happened in Bristol in 1660, the people were not always prepared to put up with attempts to abolish their favourite sports. The Justices issued a proclamation forbidding the ancient sports of cock-throwing, dog-tossing and football in the streets - they were defied and a riot took place!

By far the greatest 16th or 17th century person favouring football was a Richard Mulcaster - headmaster of Merchant Taylors and St. Paul's. This is the first evidence of it being of benefit for schoolboys to play the game - although not using the actual words, talked about the use of a coach and a referee.

In general it can be assumed that all schoolboys played football during this period, the origins were in place at Eton and Winchester. There had been little discipline and few rules in the medieval university where unruly street football was popular with the students.

At Cambridge in 1574 the Vice-Chancellor issued a decree banning scholars from playing the game within five miles of the university on pain of a fine of 6s. 8d - five years later a fight between Cambridge footballers and local players at Chesterton took place - must be one of the first away matches. Contact between locals and the university was disapproved of and all away matches were forbidden.

Football among the clergy was still a problem - young men were strongly tempted to join in the game which went on after service in the churchyard or a neighbouring field. A curate in Hawridge (Berkshire) rushed through his service to devote the rest of the time to football, his offence was more serious as he played in his shirt and was sacked by the bishop!

The restoration of the Stuarts did not mean any change to sporting activities on Sundays in the 18th century - prosecutions for Sabbath-breaking continued though less frequently. At Colne (Lancashire) in 1713 various men were in court caught playing football during service time. The whole congregation sometimes preferred football to Church attendance as may be seen at East Looe (Cornwall) in 1722 - a violent hurricane had blown down most of the steeple of the church, most of the Parishioners would have been killed but for the fact they were involved in football!

From 1722 no more is heard of Sunday football - doubtless it was still played but little attempt was made to stop it. The great controversy which had started in the second half of the 16th century which had led to the banning of Sunday football over a period of 150 years, died peacefully away at the beginning of the 18th century.

There seems to have been little opposition, though the game remained illegal until towards the end of the 18th century, councils once more found it a nuisance in the streets and a campaign of suppression was started - the creation of organised police forces gave the authorities for the first time real power to enforce their wishes.

A long running saga at Derby had started in 1731 by the mayor to abolish football - the inhabitants being very keen to play the game. The various mayors tried annually to stop it, but were not finally successful until 1847 and then only after the Riot Act had been read and cavalry sent into the town.

At Kingston-on-Thames in 1790, several people were charged with riotous conduct in playing football but had pleaded that they were celebrating the anniversary of an ancient victory over the Danes - they were acquitted.

One of the most notable riots in the history of the game took place in Lincolnshire in 1768 at Holland Fen - around 200 men played there for two hours when a troop of dragoons, some gentlemen from Boston and four constables seized some rioters, committing them to Spalding gaol. It sounds like a victory for anti-football forces, but no further action was taken, they were released on bail and several women set at liberty. When football was started on the fen two weeks later, there was no opposition.

The question now arises at this stage whether these games of football were played between definite teams or little more than a meaningless brawl but evidence for matches between teams representing parishes, villages, towns or even counties begins to start during the 1700's.

Early Barnet Football

Market Place football in 1750

University football seems to have been quiet during the 18th century when the undergraduate was becoming too sophisticated for such rude sport. At Oxford the game was forbidden under the statutes of 1636 which stopped nearly everything. Students did not become interested in football until the great revival of the 19th century - the same was no doubt the case at Cambridge.

There is a record of a football celebration at Magdalene College in 1679, to which the authorities took exception:

'That no schollers give or receive at any time, any treat or collation on account of ye football play, on or about Michaelmas Day, further than Colledge beere or ale in ye open hall, to quench their thirsts. And particularly, that yt most vile custom of drinking and spending money....'

This makes it clear that Michaelmas football and the celebrations were a well established custom, which the senior common room sought to control, not to abolish.

At Rugby, as yet unaware of the part it was destined to play later in the history of football, the first playing field was opened in 1749 and we can be sure that football was immediately played there.

The 18th century brings the first modern reference to the game at Eton and other public schools plus other types of schools - in 1766 football is listed with 33 other games popular at Eton.

It is known that football was being played at Westminster, Charterhouse was developing its unique game in Cloisters. Football also underway at Harrow and Shrewsbury, we know for certain it was played at Winchester even in the 16th century.

Throughout the early years of football history there was virtually no change or development to the game - this may seem surprising but when we consider that the Greek and Roman game of harpastum was popular for 800 years without evolving, it becomes easier to understand how our own game remained more or less the same until the 19th century. The status of the game did not always remain the same, there were changes of fashion and attitude.

The first reference to women playing football was in the 17th century at Inveresk in Scotland, when single women played against married women.

With the 19th century the speed of change quickens and in a 100 years modern football emerges with rules, its complicated organisation of leagues, professionalism and the F.A. Cup.

As a writer in 1822 in a *Gentleman's Magazine* put it - 'Football is now the most common sport, especially on Sunday afternoons'. An Etonian writing in 1831:

'I cannot consider the game of football as being at all gentlemanly. It is a game which the common people of Yorkshire are particularly partial to, the tips of their shoes being heavily shod with iron: and frequently death has been known to ensue from the severity of the blows inflicted thereby'

During the next 50 years a complete transformation took place - the rise of the public school carried its influence to the universities and was to affect the whole of English football. It would be true to say that the structure of the modern game is built on a foundation by public schoolboys of the early Victorian period.

Meanwhile the old festival game, still traditional in many towns, was coming more into collision with law and order - soon to appear in more efficient form as Sir Robert Peel's new police. Most councils lacked the power to control their unruly populations and there was insufficient public opinion to back them up. Some did succeed. At Beverley (Yorkshire) the constables tried to stop a game - they were roughly handled and the match continued; the aggressors were arrested later, tried and condemned to hard labour.

The new system, introduced by Sir Robert Peel in the 1830's gave authorities a power which they had not had before in the old days of watchmen and constables - this change had fateful consequences for Shrovetide football.

Various problems had continued over the years at Derby, including a player drowned in the Derwent river - the final stage was reached in 1845. The *Derby Mercury* had always criticised football, calling the game as 'dirty, unmanly and absurd play'; the Mayor had tried diplomacy where threats of force had failed, even to substitute athletic sports instead of a Shrovetide football match.

In 1847 the Mayor, a man of great determination, wanted to end the nuisance once and for all - nothing was left to chance this time: special constables were called out and two troops of dragoons were held in reserve. Despite the display of force, the game started as usual and when the Mayor appeared on horse-back he was stoned; so the Riot Act was read and the troops called in. Some were arrested and brought to trial, but the magistrates were lenient and the charges dismissed. Next year further trouble was anticipated and the Mayor was ready again with cavalry but it was not needed as nothing happened!

In the end, all Shrovetide and other festival matches gave way to this growing desire for public order, except in those cases where pride in the old tradition brought about a compromise in the preservation of the game - more or less a museum piece to the present day at Jedburgh (Scotland), Alnwick (Northumberland) and Ashbourne (Derbyshire).

At Ashbourne there was no opposition till 1858 in which year the Rev. J. Errington tried unsuccessfully to have the match played on Ashbourne Green instead of the Market Place - this was the start of a struggle between the players and the authorities which ended in legal proceedings. In 1860 a number of footballers were prosecuted under a section of the Highways Act - the players decided on resistance. A sum of £200 was raised for an eminent counsel, the players were convicted but an appeal was granted. Now a test case, watched by footballers in other towns, went to the Queen's Bench - judgement was given against them and the illegality of football in the streets was established. In 1862 the game started as of old in the Market Place - quickly the police made a number of arrests; after which the players came to terms and signed an agreement to play outside the town in future - an agreement still in force today.

At this period each school played its own version of the game - the form it took was dictated by the playing space available. There were four examples, the Charterhouse game in the cloister 70 yards long and 12 feet wide, a door at each end was the goal. The Eton Wall Game made to fit a playing space - in this case it cannot be older than 1717, when the wall was built. The field of play being 120 yards but only 6 yards wide - the goals consist of a garden door and part of an elm-tree marked in white, the object of each side is to get the ball into the opponent's end by means of a series of scrimmages against the wall.

Winchester football took place on a ground 80 yards by 27 yards bounded by ropes and again 3 feet outside the ropes by netting 8 feet high, there is kicking and handling allowed - very complicated rules though not unrelated to other school football. The Eton Field Game took place on a ground of various sizes, consisting of only 4 players a side, no handling or passing, more of a skill to dribble the ball towards the opponents' goal - if kicked through, 3 points are scored.

All these games were outside the main stream of evolution, at many other schools the game was based on the mass football of earlier centuries. The number of players was unlimited, there were some scrimmages and they were allowed to handle as well as kick the ball - though not as yet to run with it in their hands.

Shrewsbury had its mass football at this period. Under a Dr. Butler (headmaster) from 1798 to 1836 the game had been forbidden and played in secret, but his successor provided a field and introduced regular games three times a week. It resembled the Rugby game in its original form as the scrimmage was a main feature - the ball was kicked or dribbled, there was a strict off-side rule and a free kick for a fair catch was allowed - the game was usually played by teams of twenty.

In 1823 an important piece of football history took place - one William Webb Ellis with a disregard for the rules of football, first took the ball in his arms and ran with it, thus originating the distinctive feature of the Rugby game - a monument is erected on the Close at Rugby to note this event. At first his act was not accepted by his own school pals, though later looked upon as being inspired. Gradually this style was brought into the game but not legalised until as late as 1841.

Here we had Charterhouse, Westminster, Eton, Harrow, Winchester and Shrewsbury separated by various points of local law and tradition, but bound by the all important principle of kicking and dribbling the ball. On the other hand stood Rugby and their followers equally united in their ways of handling and running with the ball.

Five years after the Ellis episode, a Dr. Arnold became headmaster at Rugby, revolutionised the public school system and the whole attitude of the English people towards games - he welcomed football as a more suitable pastime than drinking, gambling and poaching.

Once at the universities the same youths continued to be separated from each other by their varying backgrounds and difference in laws of the game they had played at school - something had to be done if there was to be any sort of organised football.

The first step taken was at Rugby on the 7th September 1846, where *The Laws of Football as played at Rugby School* were put in place - regarded as a set of decisions on certain disputed points in football rather than containing all the laws of the game. Hacking (kicking) though not to be achieved with the heel or to parts of the body above the knee was an accepted feature of the play - later this became the subject of great controversy and was one of the causes which led to the formation of the Football Association.

Also in 1846, John Charles Thring and Henry De Winton, former pupils of Shrewsbury School, persuaded some Old Etonians to join them in forming a club. A few matches were played on Parker's Piece, Cambridge, but the club did not survive for long.

Oldest Known Football Photograph

Pictured back in 1855 is the Addiscombe (near Croydon) Military Academy team, the number of players in a side varied during this period - 16 on display this time! The Academy was set up by the East India Company and was responsible for the schooling of officers who were to serve in India under the British Empire - it closed down 5 years after this photo was taken.

The different variations of the game often resulted in confusion when teams met - some teams permitted the hands to be used and others stuck to the belief that feet only should be used. In 1848 an attempt was made to reach some sort of unity and set of rules - a number of old students from Eton, Harrow, Winchester, Rugby and Shrewsbury met at Cambridge. After lengthy discussions a list of rules was drafted and approved - these were know as *The Cambridge Rules* but nobody sadly took much notice of them. Cambridge confirm that this piece of football history does not still exist in their archives, only the later rules from 1863.

The earliest record of a football club was Surrey F.C., founded in 1849 - consisting of members from cricket clubs, Surrey, Surrey Paragon, South London and the Union. It is clear from their rules, accepting a team of up to 22 and kicking over the 'goal ropes' rather than under, that Surrey F.C. played a form of rugby and not soccer.

In its early days, football was played between sides of unlimited numbers and without any particular formation but by 1850 opposing teams usually consisted of between 15 and 20 men each.

In 1852 there was match between Yorkshire team Holmfirth v Leicestershire team Enderby at Sheffield's main sporting venue of the day, Hyde Park - for a stake of £20.

Bramall Lane opened in 1855 and was available for all sports except pigeon shooting and whippet racing! The first public event in April, was a cricket match in which William Prest played - later a founder of Sheffield F.C.

Sheffield F. C. is the World's first Association football club and would have a major impact on the history of football (See photo) - in May 1857 wine merchant William Prest and solicitor Nathaniel Creswick talked into the night about the need for an organised sport to keep these two keen cricket lovers fitness levels up during the winter months. On 24th October 1857 the Sheffield Club was formed, officials were elected with a secretary and captain and headquarters were established in a potting shed and green house of 'Parkhouse', the home of Thomas Asline Ward, at the bottom of East Bank Road.

The first job was to study the existing ways of playing football - Creswick wrote to the leading public schools, Eton, Harrow, Winchester, Westminster and Rugby and collected together the different sets of rules. Like others before them, the public school rules were almost impossible for them to understand and were meant more for people already familiar with the game. Seventeen members of the middle class club came from

Sheffield Collegiate School and would have influenced the ways of playing, together with a broader view of football, enabling them to lay down their own code of laws which became the foundation for the first common rules to be taken up by the F.A. in six years time. Messrs. Creswick and Prest went for a walk into the country to decide which rules of football they should use for the club. After much debate one of **the first major playing rules of Football were decided on 21st October 1858:**

1. Kick off from the middle must be a place kick.
2. Kick out must not be from more than 25 yards out of goal.
3. Fair catch is a catch from any player provided the ball has not touched the ground and has not been thrown from touch. Entitles a free kick.
4. Charging is fair in case of a place kick but he may always draw back unless he has actually touched the ball with his foot.
5. No pushing with the hands is allowed but no hacking or tripping up is fair under any circumstances whatsoever.
6. Holding the ball, excepting the case of a free kick, is altogether disallowed.
7. No player may be held or pulled over.
8. It is not lawful to take the ball off the ground for any purpose whatever.
9. The ball may be pushed or hit under any circumstances.
10. A goal must be kicked but not from touch nor by a free kick from a catch.
11. A ball in touch is dead, consequently the side that touches it down must bring it to the edge of the touch and throw it straight out from touch.
12. Each player must provide himself with a red and dark blue flannel cap, one colour to be worn by each side.

There is little evidence that any of the above rules were of a public school origin - young village players in the neighbouring area were persuaded away from the handling of the ball by providing them with spotless white kid gloves with silver florins to be held in their hands. If they offended, the club officials would penalise the offender by taking the coin from them!

The new club attracted a lot of local interest and as there was no immediate opposition, the members organised themselves into teams so they could play matches like Married Men v Unmarried Men, Professional Occupations v The Rest, 1st half of alphabet v 2nd half or Law v Medicine. There was no limit to the time played, or numbers of players on each side. No crossbars to the goals, which were as wide as the teams agreed upon - 12 feet up to 20 feet and corner flags were the only limit to the field of play.

The first game against external players was v the 58th Regiment, which Sheffield easily won - two of the soldiers suffered broken ribs! Early grounds where Sheffield F.C. played were in a field behind Thomas Ward's house on East Bank Road (near Sheffield Wednesday's ground at Olive Grove), the Newhall Athletic ground in the east of the city, followed by the Old Forge - during the 1860's the club struggled to find decent playing and practice grounds, which slowed the progress of the team.

In the early years of Sheffield F.C., athletics was very important - between 1858 and 1867, the biggest events were the annual sports meetings. The gate money from athletics was the main source of income for many Sheffield clubs.

Public school input was taken up by 1860 - at Eton, the scholars adopted a method of forcing a goal by having an area 4 yards on either side of the goal marked with flags to score a 'rouge'. Players were awarded a point for touching the ball down within or kicking it through these areas and was used by clubs in the Sheffield area during the 60's. It was adopted as there were many 0-0 draws, due to Sheffield's goals being only 4 yards wide. A goal outweighs any number of rouges, if the goals scored was equal, the match was decided by rouges - it did not catch on nationally and was eventually scrapped.

Matches were very private affairs, only members and their friends could enter the ground - playing members were provided with beer and tobacco at home games! In 1867, an omnibus was arranged to away matches and each player who had a dinner at another club was paid 5s. (25p)

On two occasions, Sheffield reached the 4th round of the F.A. Cup - in 1877-78 losing to the famous Wanderers by 3-0 and again in 1879-80, drawing 2-2 v Notts Forest but were disqualified.

Unlike the other two Sheffield clubs Wednesday and United, Sheffield F.C. preferred to stay an amateur team and won the F.A. Amateur Cup in 1904 v Ealing at Valley Parade, Bradford - from the cup winning side Fred Milnes was to captain the team to tour America in 1905. It was Sheffield F.C.'s 150th anniversary in 2007, one of their celebrations was a game against Inter Milan at Bramall Lane. Sheffield F.C. is one of only two clubs in the world to hold a FIFA Order of Merit, the other being Real Madrid - the club now plays in the Unibond League.

Teams of 9 forwards and two defenders came into fashion before 1860, the formation quickly developed into a combination of goalkeeper, one back, two half-backs and 7 or 8 forwards. The later Sheffield Association clubs usually preferred the 12 player team.

In 1857 'Tom Brown's Schooldays' was published. No book has done more to form a true picture of an English public school - it gave the first fictional account of English school football. The author, Thomas Hughes was at Rugby from 1834 to 1842, so the scene he paints can be taken as true for this period.

World's Oldest Football Ground

Hallam F.C. first played at their Sandygate ground in 1860

12

The Blackheath Club was founded in 1858 by old boys from Rugby, and the once famous but now long extinct, Blackheath School, but this team chose to play according to Rugby School rules.

Hallam F. C. (Sheffield) became the second football club and were formed in 1860 by Thomas Vickers and John Charles Shaw, both had been members of the Sheffield F. C., Shaw became captain of the team and later President of the Sheffield F. A. Hallam Cricket Club had been in existence since 1804, when the landlord of the 'Plough Inn' lent one of his fields for cricket matches - like Sheffield F. C., the interest for a winter sport created the football club.

Hallam's first match was v Sheffield F. C. on Boxing Day 1860 at their Sandygate ground, when darkness fell on the occasion, Sheffield were declared winners by 2-0.

Hallam's Sandygate Stadium is the world's oldest football ground (see photo), being in continuous use since 1860 - leaving in 1933 due to landlord problems, other clubs playing there but returning in 1951. Hallam now play in the Northern Counties East League. The ground is still shared with the Cricket Club, their first matches of the season being played away until the football has finished. A new main stand and small stand at one end for standing have been built in recent years together with floodlights.

By 1861, the number of teams in the Sheffield area was starting to grow - there were now eight followed by another three the following year. The Sheffield F.C. club were so strong, that they permitted any of their opponents to outnumber them on the field!

Another very early team was Forest F.C. or Forest-Leytonstone as they were often called, founded by old boys from Harrow, who began playing teams at Epping Forest (Snaresbrook).

The Rugby variety of football was well on the way to becoming the accepted public school game by 1860, but a handful of the proudest and most ancient schools resisted the rugby influence and preferred to keep the traditional forms of the game which had been developing for centuries. Charterhouse had their own rules in 1861 and Westminster theirs for example - there were now two rival ways of playing football. Whilst each thought its own form of the game superior, neither thought in terms of two separate games.

At Uppingham School (Rutland), football started in 1861 with 15 players per side (see photo). There were 4 organised matches played in that year, the goals were 6 paces wide with no fixed size of the pitch - the kick-off was a quarter of the way up the ground. The Headmaster Rev. Edward Thring, played football with the boys, but it was his brother John Charles Thring who was involved in the first Cambridge rules of 1846, in 1862 issued a code *The Rules of the Simplest Game*. These combined the best features of the two main types of football and was used at this school until the 1880s. As these are one of the earliest set of rules, they now make interesting reading:

1. A goal is scored whenever the ball is forced through the goal and under the bar, except it be thrown by the hand.
2. Hands may be used only to stop the ball and place it on the ground before the feet.
3. Kicks must be aimed only at the ball.
4. A player may not kick the ball whilst in the air.

15 Players in a Team!

Pictured in 1861, the Uppingham (Rutland) Public School team - the school became members of the F.A.

5. No tripping up or heel kicking allowed.

6. Whenever a ball is kicked beyond the side-flags, it must be returned by the player who kicked it, from the spot it passed the flag-line in a straight line towards the middle of the ground.

7. When a ball is kicked behind the line of goal, it shall be kicked off from that line by one of the side whose goal it is.

8. No player may stand within 6 paces of the kicker when he is kicking off.

9. A player is 'out of play' immediately he is in front of the ball and must return behind the ball as soon as possible. If the ball is kicked by his own side past a player, he may not touch it, kick it, or advance, until one of the other side has first kicked it, or one of his own side, having followed up, has been able, when in front of him, to kick it.

10. No charging allowed when a player is out of play, i.e. immediately the ball is behind him.

In 1862 another meeting was arranged at Cambridge. Again a new code of play was drawn up, but its fate was the same as that of 1848 and nobody took much notice of the suggested draft.

The matter was brought to a head in 1863 as a result of a series of articles in the press by a John Cartwright, in which he asked for a conference between representatives of different schools and universities to draw up a united code of rules.

The first effects were seen at Cambridge in early October 1863, where members of six schools - Shrewsbury, Eton, Rugby, Harrow, Marlborough and Westminster met to consider the subject. Of these six schools, Eton, Harrow and Westminster favoured the dribbling game - the attitude of Shrewsbury was 'mixed' and Marlborough plus Rugby the rugby code. The result was to ban some of the main features of Rugby such as hacking, tripping and running with the ball - the rugby section broke off relations with the rest and continued their own game. The end result was new regulations entitled 'Cambridge University Football Rules'.

Another early dribbling club was Crystal Palace, started in 1861 for the workers at the Palace - no connection with the present club.

Notts County were founded in 1862 as an imitation of Sheffield F.C., whose rules it adopted. Like Sheffield,

Football at Eton

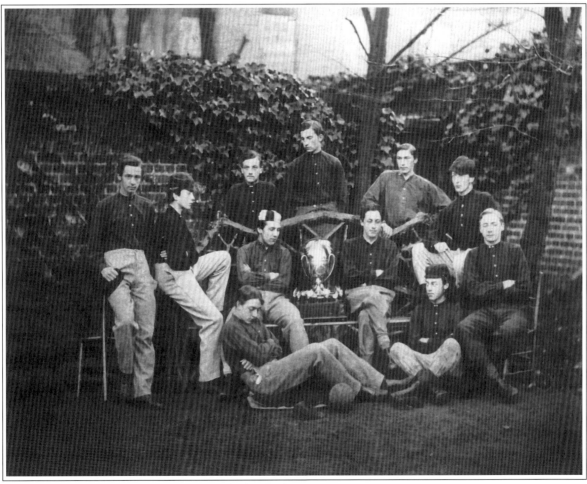

The Eton team in 1865, an important school in early football development

club members initially played games amongst themselves in The Park in Nottingham. The first official match with Nottingham Forest was a mixture of Association and Rugby. There were serious financial problems in 1881, but due to the efforts of Arthur Ashwell it was able to continue. Notts County were tenants in this year of Trent Bridge and while they were there, it became one of the greatest homes of Association Football.

In 1883, County reached the Semi-Final of the F. A. Cup, losing 2-1 to the Old Etonians at the Oval. Finalists in 1891, before winning the Cup in 1894, 4-1 v Bolton Wanderers. Great efforts were made to keep their amateur status, but they changed to professionalism in 1885 and were founder members of the Football League three years later.

Rumours in Staffordshire suggest that a form of football was known in Roman days, which was of a somewhat brutal nature! In 1863, **Stoke City** were started by some Old Carthusians - Armand, Bell, Matthews and Phillpott, pupils of the North Staffordshire Railway works. With the help of J.W. Thomas, who was connected with the Stoke Victoria Athletic Club, they started their venture. In those early days, Stoke played a modified form of Rugby, their ground being Sweetings Field. Mr. Tom C. Slaney, a schoolmaster, did a lot to place the club on its feet and became captain between 1875 to 1882.

Stoke won the Staffordshire Cup in 1878 and again the following year. In 1883 a move was made to the Victoria ground and adopting the professional code, they were admitted to the League in 1888. At this time, the players were paid 2s 6d. per match - this led to a strike because they discovered other clubs were paying 5s. per game!

There were two other dribbling clubs founded in 1863 - Barnes and the Civil Service.

There were only three clubs playing according to the Rugby rules before 1863, the oldest being the now famous Blackheath club, which unlike some of the dribbling clubs, still catered for the same middle-class and public-school type player.

While many clubs were started by groups of men already linked together by their work or school, there were others which owed their origin to an advertisement in the press by a few enthusiasts. An example which appeared in the *Leeds Mercury* - 'FOOTBALL - wanted a number of persons to form a football club for playing in Woodhouse Moor for a few days a week from 7 to 8 o'clock a.m. Apply K.99 Mercury office'. The good response led to the foundation of the Leeds Athletic Club with over 500 members, and annual subscription being 1s. - deciding to play at 6.30 a.m. every morning plus evening games as well.

By 1862, Sheffield F.C. had produced a set of printed rules based on five years of experience and used by a large number of teams in its area and were a significant part of the national game. The F. A. were ignorant of this and it was the Sheffield Secretary, Chesterman who in November 1863 made contact between the two bodies. Instead of working closely with Sheffield, the F. A. hardly interacted with anyone!

We now find ourselves standing on the threshold of the formation of the Football Association - it should be noted that the original plan was to include all features both of the dribbling and handling ways of playing football.

The representatives of eleven London clubs and schools met on October 26th 1863 at the Freemason's Tavern, London to try and establish at long last one national set of rules and governing organisation. The names at the meeting may seem unfamiliar now: N.N. (Kilburn), Barnes, War Office, Crusaders, Forest (Leystonstone), Percival House (Blackheath), Crystal Palace, Blackheath, Kensington School, Surbiton and Blackheath School - some played the dribbling and others the rugby game.

The first decision was easy, that the clubs represented at this meeting now form themselves into an Association to be called 'The Football Association'.

Several meetings were held, some of them stormily contested - both sides made concessions and what was described as a compromise was agreed. An examination of the rules adopted suggests it was more of a victory for the Blackheath Rugby group - for example that, A player may be hacked on the front of the leg below the knee while running with the ball.

A player is entitled to run with the ball in his hands if he makes a fair catch or catches the ball on the first bound.

Tripping shall not be allowed except when running with the ball.

A player may be held when running with the ball.

This basically is Rugby and found little favour with those clubs going for the dribbling game - it was an uneasy settlement and when news reached London that the Cambridge dribblers had drawn up a code of their own - no mention of running with the ball, and though charging was permitted, holding, pushing with the hands, tripping up, and shinning were out, it was decided to hold fresh meetings, to which the Cambridge committee was invited.

Classic Victorian Football Pose

Dressed a bit like 'convicts' are 12 'gentleman' players from Harrow School in 1867, the rules from Harrow spread to several parts of the country

The fifth meeting of the F. A. came in December 1863 - it was a bad tempered one and brought the rival parties a step nearer to a split. On one hand were A. Pember (President), E. C. Morley (Hon. Secretary) and J. F. Alcock who were supporting the Cambridge views and wanted the 'rugby rules' deleting from the original Draft Laws. Against them was a group led by F. W. Campbell (Hon. Treasurer) and W. H. Gordon both of the Blackheath club.

Now followed the arguments from both sides that suggested Rules 9 and 10, running with the ball and

hacking had better be considered first before any final draft was settled, because upon these two rules everything else depended.

The end result was a victory for Mr. Campbell's proposed amendment, seconded by Mr. Gordon with 13 votes to 4 that these 2 rules are deleted.

So with hostility still in the air the 6th and last act in the birth of the Football Association came on Tuesday 8th December 1863 at 7 p.m.

We can picture the setting in the old Freemason's Tavern, Greet Queen Street, Lincoln's Inn Fields, London. The room cut with shadows thrown by the oil lamps; the styles of a past age; top hats placed upon tables or hanging in the corners; cabs rattling up to the front entrance. Here were the eminent mid-Victorians, reflecting some of the heroism in the Crimean War - the proud owners of beards, back in fashion after 200 years and smoking, a habit which had gone out of favour in polite circles for the previous 80 years.

This was the background on that December evening when Campbell of Blackheath, at last arose to settle the parting of the ways. Although his club approved of the objections of the Association, the laws, he said, destroyed the game and took all interest away from it - he therefore wished their names to be withdrawn from the list of the Association's members.

Had circumstances been different and with more patient negotiation, there might have been no divide between Association and Rugby but ONE single game.

When the Rugby Union was formed in 1871 'hacking' was withdrawn from its laws, through the insistence of the same Blackheath club who had fought for it earlier!

The rules of the Football Association were soon published in the leading sporting paper of the day - *Bells Life* and a pocket book costing 6d. by Lilywhite was made available to the public - two among them were decisive:

No player shall run with the ball.

Neither tripping nor hacking shall be allowed, and no player shall use his hands to hold or push his opponent.

The Association was at first a feeble and small organisation - its original income had been from subscriptions and amounted to only £5 in 1863, in 1875 carrying a cash balance of only £2 17s. 5d. Differences of opinion led to withdrawals and refusals to join and at one time only ten members - Barnes, Civil Service, Crystal Palace, Kensington School, London Scottish (Ripley), N.N. (Kilburn), Royal Engineers (Chatham), Sheffield, Wanderers and Worlabye House (Baty's). No public school was included due to another difference of opinion - the off-side rule. Eton and Harrow wanted a strict rule, with all players in front of the ball off-side, while Charterhouse and Westminster wanted the pass forward. As before the influence of the last two schools prevailed and a solution was reached by 1867.

This decision not to adopt a rigid off-side rule decided the form Association football would take in the future. In the old dribbling game the only possible tactic was for the man with the ball to kick it in front of him towards the goal, keeping it as closely under control as possible, while his colleagues backed him up, in case he overran it or was robbed by an opponent - in effect the attack was delivered in column, instead of a line as with the modern game.

The throw in was established in 1863 by the F. A., it had been mentioned in the Sheffield laws as early as 1858 but in the majority of games previously, the ball was kicked back into play. Handling of the ball was still allowed in some matches and a kick at goal could be won by touching down over the opposition's goal-line.

The first match played under the new Association rules was on 9th January 1864 at Battersea Park, south of the River Thames - sides chosen by the Secretary and President of the F. A. After the game, the players and officials adjourned to a hotel in Pimlico to celebrate their success.

In 1865 a new rule - tape to be stretched across the goals 6 feet from the ground. The next year other changes - fair catch rule omitted, kick out rule altered and goal-kicks introduced.

Football was spelt 'Foot Ball' for sometime, showing the difference between the ball games - the use of the foot instead of the hand. The word 'soccer' comes from a 19th century altered abbreviation of 'association' as in Association Football.

The fact that stamp duty was abolished back in 1855 led to an increase in journalism - *Bell's Life* was the leading sporting paper and during the 1850s occasionally devoted a column to public school or university football and by 1860 was reporting club football - the next ten years saw a great increase in football reporting.

Football colours are an ancient idea and are first heard of on the continent 450 years ago when in Florence the players wore red and green kit respectively. The public schools were the first to adopt a kind of football outfit - long white flannel trousers and shiny black belts. Winchester had special clothes including coloured jerseys as early as 1840. Often the clothing consisted of some players in hats, long trousers, white or striped-like pyjamas and various kinds of shirts - shortly knickerbockers were worn having come into fashion. It is not known exactly when football caps were first used - probably at Rugby, and were soon widely seen.

The secretary of the FA, Mr. Alcock, found many problems at the beginning - a separate Association had been formed in Scotland and refused to allow the English to dictate, the same thing was happening in Wales and

Ireland - these countries insisted upon having rules of their own. Mr. Alcock worked very hard to restore harmony and it was not until 1882 that peace reigned.

The period following the establishment of the F.A., the rules, not to mention the size of the teams, were varied and still subject to dispute. The game remained one mainly for ex-public and grammar school boys, dominated in the 1860s by the Old Etonians (1865) and the Wanderers (1864), the latter only open to men who had attended the leading public schools.

By 1865, Sheffield F.C. were playing their first matches outside Sheffield - against Lincoln, Nottingham and Manchester. Lincoln failed to raise a team initially, many of their players preferred to watch the Lincoln races instead! Sheffield tried to promote the F. A.'s rules throughout the Sheffield region but had problems with the restrictive offside law, which had anyone in front of the ball out of play. This offside rule was abandoned in Sheffield, which persuaded the F. A. to make changes.

Nottingham Forest were founded in 1865. At first they played 'shinney' a game which is the father of modern hockey. 'Shinney' or 'bandy', as it was often called did not satisfy the young men who played this old fashioned game on the Forest Recreation Ground. A meeting resulted in the start of the Nottingham Forest F.C. The first match v their neighbours Notts County - described as a 'great fight'!

One of the first actions of the club was to buy twelve red caps with tassels - the red colour was in honour of the Italian Giuseppe Garibaldi, whose men were known as the Redshirts after the colour of their outfit.

The Foresters were for some time in the Sheffield Association and in 1879 made it to the Semi-Final of the Cup, losing 2-1 v Old Etonians and again at this stage the next year, 1-0 to Oxford University. The Cup was finally won 3-0 v Derby County in 1898 at Crystal Palace.

Sheffield Wednesday started in 1866 by a group of cricketers called The Wednesday - the day of the week in Sheffield set aside for worker's recreation who decided on forming a football club to fill in the winter months. In 1871 they settled at Bramall Lane, now home of Sheffield United, before opening the Olive Grove ground in 1887 - the previous year Wednesday turned professional.

The club was refused admission to the League but helped form the Football Alliance and joined the League when it was extended in 1892. The F. A. Cup was first won in 1896 2-1 v Wolves and again in 1907 v Everton 2-1. In September 1899, Sheffield opened their new

First Important Football Cup

The Youden Cup won by Hallam F.C. in 1867 at Bramall Lane Cricket Ground, Sheffield

ground at Owlerton and climbed back to the First Division.

Also starting in 1866 was **Chesterfield.** It was not until 1871-72 that a meeting was held and a set of rules drawn up - friendly games were played against teams like The Wednesday, Notts Forest, Sheffield Garrick and Sheffield Gentlemen. The first competition was entered in 1891, when Chesterfield won a cup given by Alfred Barnes - a large colliery owner and Member of Parliament. The next year, they won the Sheffield Cup, the Derbyshire Minor Cup and the Barnes Cup again.

In 1896 Chesterfield joined the Midland League until being elected into League Division II in 1899. The club was reconstructed in 1918, coming under control of the Corporation - the first team in the country to play municipal football.

In 1866 a letter was sent to the F.A. headquarters from the Secretary of the Sheffield F.C. Club - it suggested a match between London and Sheffield. There existed a difference between the two cities re the laws - the Sheffield off-side rule required only ONE defender between the attacker and the goal. The F.A. accepted the match should go ahead in March at Battersea Park, eleven-a-side. This was the first ever representative match played by the Football Association.

Listed below are some of the rules agreed by the two opponents:

Oldest Inter-City Matches

Sheffield v London games first played in 1866, shown is a London team from c. 1874. Back row 4th from left is C.W. Alcock (Treasurer & Secretary of F.A.), holding the ball is Hon. A.F. Kinnaird (later President, Chairman & Treasurer of F.A.)

1   The ground to be 120 yards long by 80 wide
2   Dress of the London team to be white jersey or flannel shirt and white trousers
3   The ball to be a Lillywhite's No. 5.
4   Play to commence at 3 p.m. and end at 4.30.
5   Notice of the match to be sent to *The Field, Bell's Life, Sporting Life and* the *Sportsman.*

This was the first time the type of football to be used and the length of a game was stipulated - as the match was played under F. A. rules, it helped the London team winning by two goals and four touchdowns to nil. So began a series of matches that lasted until the turn of the century, out of them grew inter-county games promoted by the F.A.

In this game, the London team saw for the first time, Sheffield players heading the ball - something never seen before in the South and one which caused some laughter! Is was not until 1875 that a Southern player took up the practice, when a Lieutenant Sim of the Royal Engineers was heading the ball in the Cup Final v

the Old Etonians - the older London players also argued against what they called 'unnecessary' passing.

Queen's Park, Glasgow were the first club in Scotland, formed in July 1867 by members of the Glasgow Y.M.C.A., other names of 'The Celts' and 'Morayshire' were considered before Queen's Park was decided. Such was their dominance, the club did not concede a goal until January 16, 1875 - the Vale of Leven broke the 7 year record.

Association Football in 1875 - a larger ball than today was used

The first county match ever played took place in the autumn of 1867, Middlesex v. Surrey and Kent - it took place again in Battersea Park among long grass and ended in a draw.

In the 1860s the formation of the team consisted of eight forwards and three defenders, a rule the F.A. changed at this time was one which made it illegal for a player to throw in from touch with one hand - some powerful players could use this style and throw the ball as far as the average player could kick!

The forwards monopolised the attack and much depended upon individual skill - a forward who could dribble well and trick his opponents was looked upon as a brilliant player, for passing was still little used.

In March 1867, representatives of 13 clubs from Sheffield met at the Adelphi Hotel to discuss the creation of a Sheffield Association. There were three rules used in Sheffield which were different from those of the F.A.: (1) Sheffield had no offside rule. (2) Sheffield gave a penalty against players for handling. (3) Sheffield counted rouges if the scores finished level. It was decided to leave Sheffield's code unchanged but acknowledged the validity of the F. A.'s rules. The following year, the long process of harmonising with the F. A. started, by deleting the use of the rouge.

There were now 15 clubs playing football in Sheffield by 1867, compared to ten teams affiliated to the F. A. - at the AGM in February this year, **but for the support from Sheffield, the F. A. had considered disbanding!**

In 1867 the world's first ever club football competition took place in Sheffield - the Youdan Cup was organised by local theatre owner Thomas Youdan. The following 12 clubs competed: Broomhall, Fir Vale, Garrick, Hallam, Heeley, Mackenzie, Mechanics, Milton, Norfolk, Norton, Pitsmoor and Wellington. The Sheffield club declined to take part in local matches but were grooming themselves for the national stage!

Oxford University Win F.A. Cup

The University defeated the Royal Engineers in 1874 & were Finalists in 1873, 1877 & 1880. This picture was taken in 1878:
Back row: E.H. Parry, H.F. Hills, H.S. Otter, J.T.Twist; Middle Row: E.H. Allington, J.H. Savory (Captain), O.R. Dunell, W.R. Page, P.J.M. Rogers; In Front: E.W. Waddington, L. Heygate

The cup final was won by Hallam 2 rouge's to nil v Norfolk, played at Bramall Lane before a crowd of 3,000, each paying 3d. admission. The Cup was presented to Hallam at a special dinner at the Adelphi Hotel and it was the club's to keep but at some stage disappeared and turned up again in 1997 at a Scottish antiques dealer, having to be bought back for £2,000!(see photo)

The Cup committee introduced extra rules - 'no waiting for players to arrive', 'the referee has the authority to award a free kick if any club makes three fouls or kicks out when the ball is thrown in, if he believe it intentional' and 'the first side to score in extra time win the match'.

By January 1868, thirty clubs had joined the Football Association - the foundations were well and truly laid and everything was ready for the huge development of the Association game.

There were old public school boys in their hundreds playing football, industrialism was making its mark on the community and it was also producing players in the Midlands and the Northern urban areas, which in fifty years changed the character of England. The introduction of the Saturday half-day had given the industrial worker a new weekly holiday - which had to be occupied. There was room for various forms of mass entertainment, one of the earliest of these was football - there was now a rapid growth of clubs in every town and village all over the country.

There was now a new football public consisting of factory workers and thousands of black-coated workers who crowded the industrial towns - it was mostly from here that the new clubs were formed in the 1870s and 1880s. To this period came many of the now famous football clubs, as well as thousands of others now forgotten or only of local importance - their humble beginnings illustrate the social revolution which was taking place. Very few of the clubs which came into existence after 1870 came from the middle classes.

Some of the developments of communications were to prove crucial to the game's growth. Football could not have grown so quickly without the expansion of the rail network.

Several clubs were still fielding sides with 15 or 20 players but the majority of teams now went for 11 or 12 men.

Walsall were founded in 1868 as Walsall Town Swifts, then Walsall Town and were later members of the Birmingham and District Football League, joining League Division II in 1892-93 before changing their name to Walsall F.C. in 1896. They first played at West Bromwich Road, moving to Fellows Park in 1900 - the club lost its place in Division II in 1901 before returning to Division III in 1921.

The goalkeeper as we know him today came into being and is in the F.A. rules of 1870 as a player who is allowed to use his hands. The word goalkeeper appeared in the Sheffield Rules before then - the relevant text appears in the rule concerning offside: 'The goalkeeper is that player on the defending side who, for the time being is nearest his own goal'.

It was about 1870 that football clubs first began to charge admission to their matches. This was not possible in earlier days when games were often played on common land or public parks. The idea of covering expenses and even making a profit by charging spectators via gate-money became the regular thing. It quickly justified itself and as the popularity of the game increased, the weekly takings of the leading clubs increased to figures unheard of before. When the first local secretary thought of collecting pennies at the gate only a few spectators filed in. However, when Aston Villa first charged for admission in 1874, the takings amounted to 5s. 3d.

At the beginning of the 1870s, the formation of a team put all the emphasis on attack - consisting of seven forwards - two played on the right wing, two on the left and three in the centre - behind them four players made three lines of defence - a goalkeeper, one full-back and two half-backs. At the end of the 70's, one of the centre-forwards was removed and a second full-back established. Dribbling of the ball had been encouraged and taught at Public Schools and most of the great players of that age came from these schools. There was some attempt at passing, but was usually as a last resort and very hit and miss - the good dribbler kept the ball as long as possible hoping to outrun the three defenders. Other players did back up the attacker, but existed more in theory than practice.

Five England v Scotland matches were played between 1870 and 1872, but only London based players took part from the two countries, so were not really recorded as true internationals.

Progress in Lancashire had been slower than London, but in 1871, the village of **Turton** (near Bolton) was the first club - started by old Harrow brothers J.C. and Robert Kay together with schoolmaster W.T. Dixon. J.C. was captain, Dixon secretary and treasurer and the Kay's father was president. Within a year their set of rules were published, clearly based on their Harrow days. The club soon had 48 playing members, mostly from the lower classes, who paid an annual subscription of 1s. - the ball they used was a cheese-shaped object!

Reading F.C. were formed in 1871 at a public meeting held at the Bridge Street Rooms. They first entered the F.A. Cup in 1877, defeating South Norwood (near Croydon) 2-0 but lost 1-0 to Upton Park in Round 2. The following year, the club amalgamated with Reading Hornets. Their initial rise to fame was winning the first Berks and Bucks Cup in 1878-79 and again in 1891-92. The club was further strengthened in 1889, when Earley F.C. joined them. Reading turned professional in 1895 and joined the Southern League - runners up in 1902-3 and 1904-05 and became founder members of League Division III in 1920. Reading reached the Semi-Final of the Cup in 1927, losing 3-0 v Cardiff City at Wolverhampton.

In 1871, the next important step in the story of football was the introduction of the F.A. Cup - founded mainly by the efforts of a C.W. Alcock, Secretary of the Football Association from 1870 to 1895. He was also a member of the Forest Club (Epping Forest), which became the famous Wanderers Club. Alcock was educated at Harrow and taken part in the Cock House competition - a system of house matches based on the knock-out idea. His fellow members at the F.A. also knew and loved these type of games.

The F.A. Cup was in effect an adaptation on a national scale of what they had known at school and Alcock found immediate support for his original proposal. A meeting took place in July 1871 at the *Sportsman* office in London - there, in an oak-panelled room, sat seven gentlemen dressed in the height of fashion matched by their place in society, each was a member of one of the best known teams of that period - Upton Park Club, Westminster School, Civil Service Club, Crystal Palace Football Club, Harrow and the Royal Engineers. After the formal business Mr. Alcock proposed: 'That it is desirable that a Challenge Cup should be established in connection with the Association, for which all clubs belonging to the Association should be invited to compete' - the idea was favourably received.

A follow up meeting was held in October attended by additional representatives from clubs Barnes, Wanderers, Harrow Chequers, Clapham Rovers, Hampstead Heathens, Windsor House Park and Lausanne - it was agreed, the rules drafted and entries were received. The first rules were simple enough, two of them read:

'The ties shall be played off within a month of the publication of the ties in such papers as the Committee may think fit, such publication to be deemed sufficient notice of the drawing'. 'In the case of a drawn match the clubs shall be drawn in the next ties or shall compete again, at the discretion of the Committee. In the event of a team refusing to play again or failing to play off the tie in which it

has been drawn, within the stipulated time, it shall be adjudged to have lost the match'

At that time there was still debate about the laws of the game, the size of the ball had to be sorted because of different local variations. It was within the power of the committee to group the teams in divisions - in the first two rounds the captains tossed for choice of ground, but all matches after that were then played at Kennington Oval.

The F.A. Cup was meant to be a challenge - the winners would be exempt from all the earlier rounds the next season and appear only in the Final, this idea was soon swept aside.

The Laws of the game as set by the F.A. when the cup began included:

1. *'The maximum length of the ground shall be 200 yards; the maximum breadth shall be 100 yards; the length and breadth shall be marked off with flags; the goals shall be upright posts, 8 yards apart with a tape across them 8 feet from the ground'*
2. *'The winners of the toss shall have choice of goals. The game shall be commenced by a placekick from the centre of the ground by the side losing the toss and the other side shall not approach within 10 yards of the ball until it is kicked off'*

You might think number two is just like today, only in 1871 there was no centre-circle and no half-way line! Every time a goal was scored, the teams changed ends - if no goals by half of the agreed time, ends to be changed. The off-side law as set by the F.A. with three players between attacker and goal, was different from that of the Sheffield Association who were ahead of their time requiring only one defender.

There were few cross-bars, no goal-nets, no free-kicks and no penalties - nor were there referees or linesmen as we know them. When the laws were established in 1863, it was assumed that they would be observed and that any infringements would be accidental - the rival captains settled all disputes in ordinary matches without delay because any offending player at once admitted a breach of the laws. When the F.A. Cup started, it was agreed to appoint two umpires, one in each half of the field and a referee to watch over the play. If the umpires could not agree a decision, an appeal was made to the referee to settle the matter.

As most of the teams fixtures lists for the 1871-72 season had already been filled, with the exception of Queen's Park Glasgow, the northern clubs were absent - Donington Grammar School (Lincolnshire) was the only other club north of Hertfordshire. Hitchin, Royal

Engineers, Reigate Priory, Maidenhead and Great Marlow were all outside the London radius, but the other eight entries - Wanderers, Harrow Chequers, Barnes, Civil Service, Crystal Palace, Upton Park, Clapham Rovers and Hampstead Heathens were all within easy reach of the City. Here were the original fifteen teams for a competition that was to become the greatest in the world.

Of the original fifteen clubs, Donington School and Hampstead Heathens received byes into the Second Round - Queen's Park were also given special consideration because of their location and travelling involved - all makes strange reading in the 21st century.

In February 1872 a sub-committee of the F.A. was appointed to select and buy the Challenge Cup. From two designs, one was selected - made of silver, it stood on an ebony pedestal and was nearly as wide as its height of 18 inches - two handles curved out of its sides and on the lid was the figure of a player. It was a modest enough trophy costing £20. Among the clubs who contributed was Queen's Park who sent a guinea, though their income for the year was only £6.

The meeting of the Wanderers and Queen's Park in the Semi-Final was the first Cup-Tie to create real interest - the Scottish were only able to travel to London with the help of public subscription. The courage of Queen's Park coming to London to challenge the mighty Wanderers was described in reports as 'the most remarkable event in modern football'. The visitors' methods were a complete revelation; they rarely tried to dribble but passed the ball with an accuracy which surprised their opponents. The Wanderers had the better of a hard game in which neither side could score, the first promise was given of Scotland's future as a football-playing race. Since they were unable to remain in London for a replay, Queen's Park retired undefeated and left the Wanderers to take a place in the first Final to meet the Royal Engineers from Chatham.

That historic game took place at Kennington Oval on March 16th 1872 before a crowd of about 2,000. The Wanderers (home ground the Oval), consisted of all the best players from Public Schools and Universities but the Royal Engineers started as favourites, having beaten Crystal Palace in the other Semi-Final and full of confidence. For the first time, and not the last, the underdogs the Wanderers won 1-0. The first Cup Final goal was scored after fifteen minutes by a A.H. Chequer, which was an assumed name taken by M.P. Betts, signifying 'A Harrow Chequer', he had been a registered member of the Harrovian Chequer club which had scratched earlier in the competition - a clear breach of the regulations! The Secretary of the F.A. was in goal for

the victorious team. The Wanderers were not presented with the Cup until 11th April at the Pall Mall Restaurant in London.

One sporting paper, *Bell's Life* reported that there were few spectators at that first Final, 'the reason being possibly that an admission of 1/- was charged'.

The Cup Final pitch was in the centre of the Oval and the ring round it was as big as a cricket ground - there were ropes around the touchlines and portable wooden stands, known as 'flower pot stands' facing the pavilion with people keen to lie down on the grass between these temporary stands and the touchline. Members of the Ground Committee used to walk over and collect half-a-crown from each person in this enclosure, stuffing the coins into their pockets and finally placing their 'treasure' on tables in the pavilion.

The corner and goal kick were introduced by the F. A. in February 1872. The Sheffield F. A., as usual leading the way, had been using these methods since 1868.

The importance of passing and combined play was being appreciated, Queen's Park and other Scottish clubs were the first to demonstrate the art - it was first used in England by the Sheffield teams and the Royal Engineers. As the combined game developed, so a greater pressure was put onto the defences - the *pure and simple* dribbler slowly went out of the game. The individual became more a team member and the speed of football increased.

Darwen FC, was established in 1872 by three brothers who were Harrow old boys - within the next three or four years a number of clubs were established in the Blackburn, Bolton and Darwen areas - matches were played according to the Association Rules.

For the 1872-73 season we see the introduction of free-kicks for handling the ball, an adoption from the rules of some Public Schools in earlier years.

England's first full international took place in November 1872 v Scotland at the West of Scotland Cricket Ground, Partick. The England players wore white shirts with three red lions, but the rest of the outfit was of their original university colours complete with caps, as heading still rarely happened. The team consisted entirely of Old Boys of the leading schools which favoured the dribbling code, it would have been unthinkable for one who was not a 'gentleman' to represent the national side! The first England captain was Cuthbert Ottaway, who played for Oxford University and cricket for Middlesex but died at the age of only 27 - he caught a chill after a night out dancing!

Cambridge University in 1882

Cambridge reached the Semi-Final of the F.A. Cup in 1877, losing to the famous Wanderers 1-0

Blackburn Rovers Win F.A. Cup For First Time

The Rovers team back in 1884: Back row: Lofthouse, McIntyre, Beverly, Arthur, Suter, Forrest, R. Birtwhistle (Umpire); Front row: Douglas, Sowerbutts, Brown, Inglis, Hargreaves. The captain is holding the original F.A. Cup, other Cups; Left: East Lancashire Charity Cup; Right: Lancashire Cup.

Even though Scotland played a 2-2-6 formation and the English 1-1-8, the game amazingly ended 0-0! Cricket was more popular in Scotland then and Queen's Park were responsible for selecting the Scottish team who played a passing game. A crowd of 2,000 paid 1/- each , with a charge of £15 for use of the ground. A photographer was due to record the event but wanted a guarantee that he would be able to sell his prints. This was not forthcoming, so he did not bother turning up! There were no pictures either of the return match at the Kennington Oval - the players kept pulling faces at the photographer, which put him off his work!

This season the Wanderers got their name onto the Cup, and being the holders, were exempt until the Final - (this is the only occasion when the holders didn't take part until the final) against Oxford University who should have met Queen's Park in the Semi-Final - once again the Scottish Club had been given a bye, but could not make the trip to London because of business engagements of some of their members. The Final of 1873, at the choice of the holders, took place for one time only at the Lillie Bridge ground at West Brompton (near Stamford Bridge).

The kick-off at the second Final was timed for 11 a.m., to enable players and their friends to watch the Boat Race which took place on the same day. Even though football had become an important sport, the rowing event was viewed as more important - in those carefree bygone days, the game began half an hour late!

The Wanderers won this time by 2-0 before a crowd of 3,000. Hon. A.F. Kinnaird scored one of the goals and was making the first of nine appearances in the Final - as he took the field ready for battle, shoulder charges freely and vigorously given and taken with some friendly hacking thrown in. Kinnaird, a half-back, wore long white flannel trousers, his jersey and a blue and white quartered cricket cap plus being the proud owner of a splendid red beard. He was on the winning side five times and on one occasion stood on his head for joy in front of the pavilion at the Oval after the Old Etonians beat Blackburn Rovers.

Lord Kinnaird served the Football Association for 55 years. Elected to the committee in 1868, he became Honorary Treasurer in 1877 and President in 1890 until his death in 1923.

1873 saw the first ever overseas tour by a football club, when the Old Etonians crossed the Atlantic to play Yale University under the rules of the English F. A. At first it looked like the Association game would get established in America, but they did not take to it. In 1875 Harvard had been trying the Rugby game, which eventually spread to end up as their own version of American Football.

In March 1873, the Scottish Football Association was formed following a meeting at a temperance hotel in Bridge Street, Glasgow. Like the English, the Association began in a small way - the pioneer clubs being Queen's Park, Clydesdale, Dumbreck, Vale of Leven, Eastern, 3rd L.R.V., Rovers and Granville. It was not long before other clubs joined and during the first year the following became members: Alexandra Athletic, Southern, Blythswood, Western, Renton, Dumbarton and Kilmarnock.

The credit balance at the end of the first year was only £1 11s. 4d. The Association soon realised that one of the first jobs was to provide a trophy for the Cup competitions which they had started - an appeal was made to the clubs and a trophy was bought for £56 12s 11d along with eleven silver-gilt and gold badges.

The Scottish F.A. remained at its humble place of birth, for which the modest sum of 3s. per night was charged - then moving to Dundas Street, Carlton Place and Waterloo Street until 1899.

In Wales at this time, most of the football was played in the north. The earliest club to form was The Druids, they played at Plasmadoc Park, Ruabon. Wrexham were founded soon afterwards in 1873.

Port Vale started in 1874 at Middleport (near Burslem) and takes its name from a house in that district - the club was first known as Burslem Port Vale playing on grounds at Morland Road, Burslem and later moving to the Cobridge Ground at Stoke. The club were members of the Football Alliance and Midland League before being elected to Division II in 1892. The next venue change was the Recreation Ground, Bryan Street, Hanley. In October 1919, Port Vale took over Leeds' fixtures after the Yorkshire club were expelled from the League.

The next season the number of entries for the Cup had jumped from 15 to 28 clubs and the Wanderers had to start in round one, although their opposition in the first two rounds both withdrew!

In the First Round we find two sides as far apart as Sheffield and Shropshire Wanderers, who after two drawn matches decided the matter by the toss of a coin - Sheffield being victorious.

Umpires, who previously been the subject of a friendly arrangement between captains, now for the first time were officially recognised in the Laws of the Game to send a player off who persistently broke the laws. The scope of the free-kick was enlarged - it was now awarded against interference with play, when in an off-side position and encroaching when a free-kick by the other side was being taken.

Aston Villa Win the Birmingham F.A. Challenge Cup

Only 6 years after the club started in 1880: Back row: J. Hughes (Umpire), W. McGregor (Vice-President & later founder of Football League), W. Mason (Secretary), E.B. Lee, H. Simmonds, T. Park, E. Davies, F. Johnstone (Vice-President), H. Jeffries (Treasurer), W. Ellis (President), Archie Hunter, C. Johnstone. Front: D. Law, H. Ball.

Earliest Known Photo of a Football Match

'Gentlemen' players of Association Football c. 1880 - the art of tackling!

Shinguards were invented in 1874 by a Samuel Widdowson, the Nottingham Forest forward who played for England. Adapted from cricket pads, and were worn outside the socks until about 1900! They were first used in 1874 by the Nottingham club but not mentioned in the rules until 1880.

More leisure time was becoming available for most people, textile workers were granted, via Parliamentary legislation, a 56 hour week with a one o'clock Saturday finish, completing a Saturday reduction begun in 1847 - others as a result of individual agreements between employers and workers. The most dramatic increases in the growth of the holiday was between 1872 and 1874, it was hardly surprising that the Lancashire textile area was to be a major early focus of working-class soccer. Free time without money was of little value in spreading the game, but there was a big rise in wages in the later part of the 19th century.

Blackburn Rovers were started in 1874 by two old boys of Blackburn Grammar School, Arthur Constantine and John Lewis. The club played at first in a field with a pond in the middle, it was thought undesirable that players should go round or through it, so was covered by planks on which turf was laid! Two years later a move was made to Alexandra Meadows, where a match was played v Partick Thistle before a crowd of 5,000. In season 1879-80, the club entered both the F.A. and Lancashire Cups for the first time.

The F.A. Cup was won by Blackburn in three consecutive years - 1884-86 and again in 1890 and 1891. Ewood Park was taken on a ten years lease in 1890 and £1,000 was spent on it and in season 1893-94 the ground was purchased for £2,500. Blackburn were League Champions in 1911-12 and 1913-14.

The great majority of new clubs were connected with people who had never been to a public school or even a grammar school and were on the wrong side of the line which divided 'gentlemen'.

In Cheshire, the first Association clubs to be formed date back to the early 1870s - from Northwich there was a Hare and Hounds team who played games of Rugby and Association Football. At Chester in October 1874 there was reported a game King's School lost 4-0 at Chester College - a defeat due to the fact that the school team did not understand the Association rules! Popular games played in the city of Chester were quoits - a heavy flat iron, rope or rubber ring thrown to encircle a peg, skittles, rugby and cricket.

In 1874 Northwich Victoria (named after Queen Victoria) was established - no doubt the Association game was played in the county before then, but some of the first records start in that year - a match between Stedman (Sandicroft) College at Comberbach v Northwich Victoria was played on a field adjoining the college - the Vics won 1-0. There were such few soccer teams in the area that the following season Northwich played only seven matches!

Macclesfield Town's origins go back to a rugby club founded c. 1850 by Col. J.W.H. Thorpe -Macclesfield F.C., who played on a field off Victoria Road called Bowfield Lane. In 1874 the club changed to the Association game, which makes them the equal oldest team in Cheshire with Northwich Victoria. The club also moved to Rostron's Field, near to Coare Street, after a few seasons moving back to Bowfield Lane.

In the early days Macclesfield played friendly matches with teams from Stoke, Congleton, Crewe, Leek and Stockport before joining the Football Combination for season 1890-91. At this time a crowd of 200 with receipts of £5 were considered good. The players were all amateurs, providing their own kit and travelling expenses.

The club engaged the services of a Mr. John Alcock, landlord of the 'Oxford Road Tavern', to supervise the training for the Cheshire Senior Cup Final. Unheard of for the period, the players were on diets, no smoking, country walks and Turkish Baths to improve their fitness! The end result a 4-1 win for Macclesfield. In 1895 Mr. Alcock was to walk backwards from Macclesfield to Buxton in two hours 43 minutes!

In September 1891 the club moved to its present home at Moss Rose, in spite of the critics who objected to the proximity of a public house! In 1895, they were incorporated into a limited company under the name Macclesfield Football and Athletic Club Ltd - in April 1897 the club was declared bankrupt. The ground was taken over by Hallifield F.C., changing their name to Macclesfield F.C. in 1899.

After World War 1, the club was reformed and joined the Cheshire League, where Macclesfield played for many years.

Macclesfield were founder members of the new Northern Premier League in 1968, later taken into the Football League by Sammy McIlroy in 1997.

Bolton Wanderers were founded in 1874 by Ogden, a schoolmaster and member of Christ Church Sunday School as Christ Church F.C. with a subscription payable by its members being one penny. As the club started without funds, each member paid 6d. for the purchase of a ball. Members of Turton F.C. helped start the football team. The Rev. Wright became President and Ogden the captain and they kept a strong grip on the club - meetings were held at Christchurch School, the vicar stipulating that the club was forbidden to assemble without him! The players came to resent this supervision and relocated itself at the 'Gladstone Hotel' - on 28th August 1877 becoming Bolton Wanderers. The team used a mixture of playing rules, mainly those of Harrow School and the F. A.

Bolton played on several grounds, including a cemetery, before settling at Burnden Park in 1895. The first game in this new stadium was a benefit match for D. Jones v Preston. The club's first major honour was winning the F.A. Cup in 1923.

Aston Villa was a nonconformist foundation, having originated with the Wesleyan chapel at Villa Cross, Handsworth, Birmingham. Their first ground was rented at £5 yearly from a butcher and their changing room from a publican at Wellington Road, Perry Barr - the first gate amounted to 5s. 3d in a match v a rugby team called Aston Brook St. Mary's, one half played under rugby rules and the other Association. The Birmingham Cricket and Football Club, which played on the Lower Aston Grounds, had most of the local support. The Birmingham and District Cup was won in 1880 (see photo).

George Ramsay came along and brought Glasgow-type football to Birmingham and he established the Villa. The landlord had a knack of asking for more rent as the finances of the club improved, so eventually a move was made to the Lower Aston Grounds - the 'pitch' officially opened Easter 1897 - this ground is now Villa Park. Villa were F. A. Cup winners in 1887, defeating neighbours West Brom 2-0 - more Cup wins followed in 1897, 1905, 1913 and 1920 and they won the League for the first time in 1893-94.

The Royal Engineers carried out the first football tour in history, three days of games at Sheffield, Derby and Nottingham - winning every match.

In 1875 the changing of ends after scoring a goal was abolished , crossbars were allowed in preference to a tape, but not initially compulsory until the international conference in Manchester in 1882. As far back as 1863, the Secretary of Sheffield F.C. wrote to the F. A. stating that crossbars were being used in their matches - in view of the disputes whether the ball had gone under the tape, it was surprising the authorities were so slow to appreciate their value for so many years!

Birmingham City were formed in 1875 (the same year as the Birmingham County F. A. started) as Small Heath Alliance by Messrs. Edmunds, the three brothers Edden and the two brothers James - the previous year there was only one club in the city, within two years there were about twenty. They could not afford to pay rent for a ground and played on waste land near Arthur Street, not far from the present St. Andrews stadium. In 1877 the club moved to Muntz Street and rented a ground for £5 from September to April. Small Heath Alliance became professional in 1884 as many of the players were working men who could not afford to lose the half day football involved.

Sheffield v Glasgow Match in 1880

Pictured are the Sheffield (dark shirts) & Glasgow (hoops) teams - they first played each other in 1874 - no shortage of officials!

In 1888 they became the first limited company and 'Alliance' was dropped, finally becoming Birmingham in 1905 - moving to St. Andrews on Xmas day 1906.

The first occasion extra time was played in a Cup Final was in 1875, when the Royal Engineers drew 1-1 with the Old Etonians.

In January 1876, a few Welsh football enthusiasts met at the 'Wynnstay Arms Hotel', Wrexham to discuss the possibility of arranging an International match with Scotland - they also decided to form the Football Association of Wales. The game with Scotland took place at Glasgow in March, with Wales losing 4-1 but the match served to increase Welsh interest and the Association was firmly established at a meeting in Shrewsbury in May 1876.

Professionalism was still illegal, so it is impossible to know exactly when payment was first made to players. However it is likely that Peter Andrews of Sheffield's Heeley club and J.J. Lang of rivals The Wednesday became the first professionals in the 1876-77 season. Lang, who on retirement was found to be blind in one eye, was an early example of a player being attracted from Scotland and given a job in a knife-making works by the club. Another Scot, F. Suter came south in 1879 to play for Darwen and no doubt paid! The problem with professionalism in football arose from the offence caused to mainly upper-middle class people, especially those with public school educations, for whom the threat to the amateur game carried a social challenge as much as a sporting one.

Manchester United's Ground Before Old Trafford

Newton Heath (Manchester United) played at Bank Street, Clayton from 1893-1910

Middlesbrough F.C. was conceived at a tripe supper at the Coronation Hotel in 1876 and born a few weeks later at the 'Albert Park Hotel' - playing its first match on the old Archery ground in Albert Park on 3rd March 1877. In their early days Middlesbrough were nomads, their pitches including Grove Hill, Middlesbrough Cricket Field and Linthorpe Road. The 'Boro won the Amateur Cup in 1895 and 1898 and were Northern League Champions in 1894, 1895 and 1897.

The club turned professional in 1889, but three years later returned to their amateur status with big money problems - finally adopting professionalism in 1899 and were voted into Division II.

The next three years 1876-78 saw the game spread rapidly. Associations were formed in Birmingham and Lancashire. Birmingham took the bold move of taking on London in a challenge match. The game was played at the Oval and easily won by the Londoners 11-0. Two years later Birmingham were back for a re-match and won 2-0, showing how quickly football had grown in that city.

In 1876 the Druids became the first Welsh club to enter the F.A. Cup - it was the year the Wanderers won the cup for the third time beating the Old Etonians 3-0 after the first game ended 0-0.

Manchester United in Cheshire for F.A. Cup Training 1909

From Left to right: Unknown, George Stacey, Tom Wilcox, Harold Halse, Harry Moger, Charlie Roberts, J. Ernest Magnall (Manager), Vince Hayes, Billy Meredith, Sandy Turnbull, Jack Pickin, James Turnbull, Alex Bell, Dick Duckworth, George Wall and Fred Bacon (Trainer).

Accrington Fixture Card for 1878-79 shows games v Blackburn Rovers & Church F.C. played under Electric Light

This year saw the start of the Shropshire, Staffordshire and Surrey County F. A.'s, among the first County organisations to appear.

Wolverhampton Wanderers originated from schoolboys from St. Luke's, Blakenhall and first played at Goldthorn Hill. Nearby, a cricket club called Blakenhall Wanderers had a football section, several St. Luke's players played for the cricket team and before the 1879-80 season the two amalgamated and Wolverhampton Wanderers were born. Until the early 1880s the top team in this area was Stafford Road, but in 1884 Wolves beat them 4-2 in a Cup match at their new ground in Dudley Road. Wolves were founder members of the Football League in 1888.

The move to Molineux in 1889 stimulated the club to new heights, reaching the Cup Final in that year, losing 3-0 to Preston before winning the Cup for the first time in 1893 1-0 v Everton.

The Welsh Cup was established in 1877, when the F. A. of Wales paid £170 for a trophy to be competed for by clubs in the country and the border counties. First winners Wrexham, defeated Druids 1-0 at Acton Park, Wrexham. So short of money, the Welsh F. A. could not present winners medals until one year later!

Crewe Alexandra's foundation date is 1877. The original Crewe Alexandra Club was formed in 1866 as a cricket club - Rugby football was the only style played in the district at that time. At a meeting held on August 21st 1877, it was decided to form an Association football club as part of the cricket club, the first secretary was a Mr. R. Bates.

The first match played at Crewe was on December 1st, 1877 v Basford, who were then the top North Staffordshire team. The first success was winning the Crewe and District Cup in 1887. Later the same season the club won the Cheshire Senior Cup - crushing Chester F. C. by 9-0. The game was staged at the Alexandra Cricket Ground on March 24th 1888 before a crowd of 4,000 - the *Chester Chronicle* describing the Chester team as '*eleven men croaking with fear, inspired by a feeling of terror, trampled on and outplayed*'.

This turned out to be a very successful season for Crewe, in addition to these local cup victories, for the only time in their history, they reached the Semi-Final of the F. A. Cup. In the second series of games 1st round Crewe 1 Derby County 0, 2nd round Middlesbrough 0 Crewe 2, before losing 4-0 v Preston, who were then one of the top teams in the country.

In one of the earlier rounds of the F. A. Cup this season, Crewe v the Swifts at Kensington, there was an incident

It was at this time a big step forward was taken, the Sheffield Association and the Football Association at last reached agreement - the 26 member Sheffield Association had kept its distance from the F.A. until 1877 but now agreed to abandon its own version of the offside rule and change to the national body. A few clubs continued to play under a variety of rules in order to play in particular games, with the captains agreeing before the action started. The habit of playing one match under Rugby rules and the return under Association, or even using one code for one half and swapping at half-time, was common well into the 1870s.

In 1877 there was a change to the throw in rule, the throw could now be in any direction - it no longer had to be at right angles. Charles Alcock saw this as a way to make the game faster - not initially adopted in Scotland. Heading was being introduced as another option and was seen as an essential skill by the mid-1880s, which in turn led to more accurate crossing from the wings.

which went down in football history. The Swifts won 3-2, but a protest was made by Crewe after the match that the crossbar at one end was 2 inches below the height required by the laws - at the inquiry it was established that at least one Crewe official knew of the error before the game, as they had checked the goals with a two-foot rule! The committee had to enforce the laws strictly and ordered the match to be replayed. Crewe were severely censured for keeping this little 'insurance' up their sleeves. It led to new Rule 28 whereby *'any protest relating to the ground, goal-posts etc., must be reported to the referee before the match begins'*.

In August 1889, a public meeting was held at the Mechanics Institute, chaired by Mayor Knott who had received a deputation from Crewe Alexandra which expressed the view that *'it was a necessity that they should seek some outside assistance and in the present state of the competition this could not be done without paying men for their services'*. The club were granted public money, so that the football clubs funds would not be touched! During this period, local lad J. H. Pearson was capped for England. In later years he refereed an F. A. Cup Final.

Crewe joined the new Football Alliance as professionals for season 1889-90, then became founder members of the new Division II in season 1892-93, but were not re-elected in 1896. The club was back in the League in 1921, when Division III (North) started up and has been in the Football League ever since.

In the early years of the F.A. Cup, the most successful teams were the Royal Engineers and Oxford University - each of which won the Cup once and appeared in the final several times between 1871 and 1877. The competition was really dominated by a team of ex-public school boys tied to no particular school or locality, known as the Wanderers, who won the cup no less than five times in the first seven years.

A number of Old Boys clubs were emerging and over the next few years came to take charge of the competition, eventually eclipsing the Wanderers, who were losing their best players and soon vanished from the scene. One of the most important Old Boys clubs were the Old Etonians, who won the cup twice and appeared in the final four times in six years.

England suffered their biggest defeat v Scotland, 7-2 at Old Hampden in March 1878.

The Lancashire F. A. was founded in 1878 under the Presidency of the Marquess of Hartington, all 28 founder members came from just six neighbouring east Lancashire towns: Blackburn, Bolton, Church, Darwen, Haslingden and Rawtenstall - no clubs yet from Manchester. The Lancashire Cup got under way the following season and like the F. A. Cup did much to encourage interest in football.

Manchester United can trace their origins back to the late 1870's. Rugby was the first type of football played in Newton Heath from the 1870's but by the end of 1880, the Association game was taking over. On the north-east of the city were the waggon works of the Lancashire and Yorkshire Railway Company, one or two areas of 'nervous' grass struggled to show the remains of the Heath where rugby had been played.

The Dining Room Committee had formed the Newton Heath (L.Y.R.) Cricket and Football Club in 1878, the first recorded game was in November 1880 v Newton Heath Wanderers losing 6-0. The ground was poor, even by the standards of the 80's - ashes had been laid that became hard as iron and thick with mud in places. There was no changing room and the players used the limited facilities first at the 'Three Crowns' in Oldham Road, then the club HQ at the 'Shears Hotel' - a half-mile from the North Road ground where around 2,000 fans appeared for matches - a stand was finally built in 1891 to hold 1,000 spectators.

The first recognition for the club was in 1884. Black, a full-back, was selected to play for Manchester & District v Liverpool at Bootle Cricket Ground. In 1889, Newton Heath L.Y.R. joined the Football Alliance, one step down from the Football League. The club finished season 1891-92 second to Notts Forest.

There was now a Manchester Football Association with its own Cup competition, later known as the Manchester Senior Cup - teams competing included: Hurst, Manchester, West Manchester, Denton, Hooley Hill, Royton and West Gorton. Newton Heath L.Y.R. were early winners of this Cup in 1886, 1888, 1889, 1890 and 1893.

For season 1892-93, the L Y.R. was dropped from the Newton Heath name and the club were elected into the Football League. A Second Division was formed but the club went into Division I as it was extended by two clubs, the other team added was Notts Forest. In October, the players training included hammer-throwing. Stewart, a large centre-half, let the hammer go without seeing his centre-forward Donaldson - the hammer hit him, 'causing the unfortunate player to fall down insensible'!

Newton Heath's early colours were green and gold, changing briefly to white shirts and blue shorts in 1896, before the famous red shirts and white shorts were adopted in 1902. For season 1893-94, Newton Heath moved to Bank Street, Clayton (see photo), more space than North Road but the windward side of the chemical works! By 1904, a crowd of 40,000 packed the

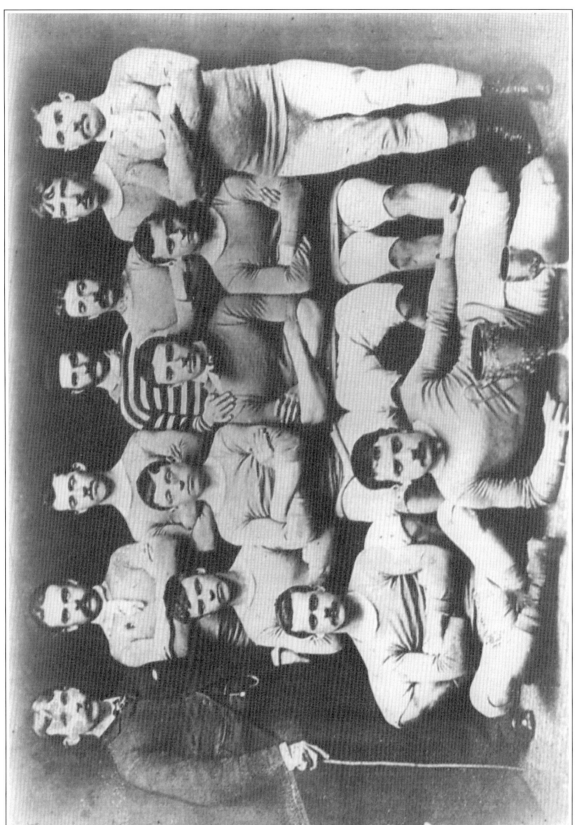

The Blackburn Olympic team who defeated the Old Etonians in 1883

enclosure v Arsenal and later the ground was selected for a representative match for the first time - English v Scottish Leagues.

In 1902, Newton Heath became Manchester United, other names considered were Manchester Celtic or Central - creditors were looking at making the club bankrupt after improvements to the ground. The club had shareholders from 1892 but never able to pay a dividend, three business men injected £500 each to keep the club going. United were League Champions for the first time in 1907-08 and F.A. Cup winners in 1909.

Prior to the Cup win, the club chose to train in 'pure' Cheshire air at the 'Bluecap Hotel', Sandiway (see photo) - a good idea as they beat Bristol City 1-0 at Crystal Palace.

United left the smells of Clayton in January 1910, the last gate only 5,000 and moved to Old Trafford. Built at a cost of £60,000, the first game was watched by 50,000 fans v Liverpool - admission charges were 6d., covered stand 1/-, 1/6 and 2/- plus limited reserved seats in the centre of the stand at 5/-.

The first ever football match to be played under floodlights took place at Bramall Lane, Sheffield on October 14ᵗʰ 1878. The teams taking part were chosen by the Sheffield Association from local clubs. The game attracted a lot of attention for electric light was still a novelty in the provinces. The official attendance was 12,000, but it is estimated at least another 7,000 gained admission without paying! The Cup Final of this year attracted only 5,000 people, so a crowd of nearly 20,000 was quite amazing. The lighting was considered a great success, the power was generated on the ground by two portable engines , one behind each goal driving Siemens dynamos. The lamps were erected on wooden towers in each corner of the ground, 30 feet high - the power of each lamp was 8,000 standard candles.

The result of the match was a 2-0 win for the team captained by W. E. Clegg, an England international, later Sir William Clegg and Lord Mayor of Sheffield - the losing team was captained by his brother J. C. Clegg, also an England international and who later became Sir Charles Clegg. Sir Charles was connected with the Football Association for 51 years. He became a member of the F. A. Council in 1886, in 1889 he was elected a Vice-president and the following year became Chairman. Finally in 1923 Sir Charles Clegg became President, a position he held until his death.

London was beaten by only three weeks for the distinction of staging the first floodlit game at the Kennington Oval on November 4ᵗʰ - the Wanderers met Clapham Rovers, but this was not as successful as the Sheffield event.

I assume a coincidence, but on the same date November 4ᵗʰ there was also a floodlit game at Accrington v Blackburn Rovers, followed by another match under lights v Church F.C. nine days later - both these events are shown on the Accrington Fixture Card for the 1978-79 season. (see photo)

The referee's whistle was tried for the first time in 1878 when Nottingham Forest were at home to Sheffield Norfolk.

When the Wanderers won the F.A. Cup again in 1878, beating the Royal Engineers 3-1, the Cup became their property, by the rules of the Competition, having been victorious three times running. However, the Wanderers gave the trophy back to the F.A. on the condition that it was not to be won outright in future by any club.

Everton were founded in 1878 from a church Sunday school, at first known as St. Domingo, their matches being played in the adjoining Stanley Park - a year later to change its name to Everton. In 1883-84 the club took an enclosed ground nearby Priory Road, for the opening match 13s. was taken. 1884-85 saw the club playing at Anfield Road, Liverpool's present ground before moving to Goodison Park in 1892, previously known as Mere Green. Everton were original members of the Football League in 1888 and won the Cup for the first time in 1906, 2-0 v Newcastle at Crystal Palace.

Dixie Dean had joined from Tranmere and aged only 19 in 1926 broke his skull and jaw in a motorcycle accident and was unconscious for 36 hours. His amazing recovery saw him score in the First Division, a League record 60 goals in the 1927-28 season - also together with F.A. Cup, Inter-League, International trial and Internationals, Dixie Dean had an amazing total of 82 goals! (see photo)

W. ('Dixie') Dean, Everton's record goal scorer

Grimsby Town were formed at a meeting at the 'Wellington Arms' in September 1878, when a group of mainly schoolmasters, doctors, solicitors and tradesmen launched it as Grimsby Pelham - a name taken from the family name of the Earls of Yarborough. Feeling the name not adequate, the following year its present name was adopted. In the fourth year of the club's existence, they entered the F.A. Cup - in 1889, when still amateurs, they gave the mighty Preston the fight of their lives at Clee Park. Grimsby joined the Football Alliance in 1889 and moved to a new ground at Abbey Park. They joined League Division II in 1892, which required a better quality ground - Blundell Park, which was not in Grimsby but in Cleethorpes.

Manchester City - Cup Winners for First Time In 1904

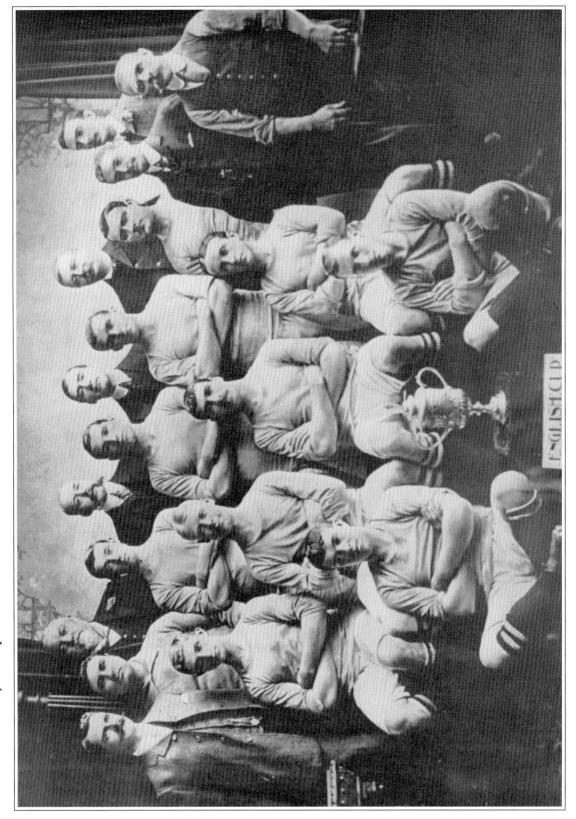

Back row: J. Parlby, C.H. Waterhouse, E. Hulton (Chairman), J.E. Chapman, G. Madders; Second row: T.E. Maley (Secretary & Manager), J. Hillman, C. Livingstone, J. McMahon, T. Hynds, W. Gillespie, L.W. Furness, J. Broad (Trainer); Third row: F. Booth, S. Frost, W. Meredith (Captain), S. Ashworth; Front row: A. Turnbull, H. Burgess.

Everton Cup Winners 1933

Back row: H. Cooke (Trainer), Britton, Cresswell, Sagar, Cook, White, Thomson. Front row: Geldard, Dunn, Dean, Johnson, Stein, Critchley.

West Bromwich Albion 'Training Walk'

Pictured in 1903 - Left to right: Shinton, Bradley, Barber (trainer), Stringer, Pennington, Simmons, Manners, Young, Haywood.

In the season 1878-79 the once mighty Wanderers lost 7-2 to the Old Etonians. For the first time northern clubs began to make their presence felt, Notts Forest reached the Semi-Final but the team to grab the headlines was the unknown outfit of Darwen - composed mainly of working young men employed in the mills of that small Lancashire town. They reached the 4th Round to play the Old Etonians at the Oval. The club could not afford the long journey to London and public money were raised. With fifteen minutes left Darwen were losing 5-1, but remarkably pulled it back to 5-5 - the battered Etonians declined the offer of extra time. So once again the long journey back to London, a sum of £175 was raised, the F.A. coming up with £10 plus £5 from the Old Etonians themselves! Another draw, this time 2-2 but a week later well beaten 6-2 - the start of Northern clubs being put on the map.

In the Darwen team were two 'mysterious' characters, James Love and Fergus Suter - Scotsmen from Partick, Glasgow. What were Scotsmen doing playing football in Lancashire? Having made visits in matches played between Scottish and English clubs, they saw, in the industrial North, better opportunities for work and wages than at home. Bringing with them the style of the Scottish game which, with its close control was in many ways superior to the English game, transforming the little Darwen side.

Having seen all the travelling by Darwen, for season 1879-80 the F.A. grouped early entries for the Cup into Divisions to reduce the long and expensive trips to London.

Among the Lancashire clubs of 1879 was one from Manchester. On March 1st Manchester Wanderers drew 2-2 with the famous Blackburn Rovers. The Wanderers had some excellent players who were included along with players from Turton, Blackburn and Accrington in the County team v Ayrshire next year.

On March 8th 1879, Cheshire played Lancashire for the first time under Association rules at Turton. Cheshire losing 6-2 and in the return match at Northwich the same month, Cheshire lost by 2-1.

As some rules in the early years of the dribbling and handling game overlapped, it is not surprising that some players were internationals at both football and rugby. The first of these was R.H. Burkett (Clapham Rovers) who first played rugby for England v Scotland, before playing soccer in 1879 v Scotland.

In 1879 the Scottish Cup was awarded to Vale of Leven, when Glasgow Rangers failed to turn up for the Final replay! The first game ended 1-1, but Rangers had a goal disallowed for offside. They appealed against the referee's decision, claiming they had won 2-1 and refused to take part in the replay.

This season also saw a change to the laws of the game. Two years earlier it was ruled a player was allowed to charge an opponent if he was facing his own goal - this led to some vigorous encounters - the law now stated 'no player shall charge his opponent by leaping on him'.

Sunderland were founded in 1879 at a meeting in the Adults School, Norfolk Street under the leadership of Scottish schoolmaster James Allan. He worked at Hendon Board School, the team started as Sunderland and District Teachers Association FC, but changed to their present name in 1881. In 1887, Robert Thompson J.P. became President and Sunderland's team was mainly composed of Scotsmen and quickly became the most formidable outfit in the county of Durham - their main rivals being Middlesbrough and Newcastle West End.

Sunderland were League Champions in 1891-92, 1892-93, 1894-95, 1901-02 and 1912-13. Season 1896-97 was a bad season for Sunderland and they lost some support and left their ground at Newcastle Road and moved to Roker Park (see photo).

West Bromwich Albion were established in 1879, when a number of employees of Salter's spring works and associated with a cricket club decided to take up a winter game. The club was first called West Bromwich Strollers. They paid 6d entrance fee and a weekly subscription of 2d, playing on an open field. The following year the name changed to Albion and played in a public park, before in 1881 they secured their first private ground, which the players enclosed themselves. A year later they moved to Four Acres, in 1885 to Stoney Lane and finally in 1901 to the Hawthorns. The first club colours were maroon, changing to the navy blue and white striped shirts in 1885.

West Brom's progress was amazing. They entered the Cup in 1883-84 and just two years later reached the first of their consecutive finals - beating Preston at their third attempt - the Cup was won again in 1892.

Doncaster Rovers were originally formed in 1879 to play a match v the Yorkshire Institute for the Deaf and Dumb. Friendly games were played until 1888, when they joined the Midland Alliance. In 1891 Doncaster became members of the Midland Counties League and this season won the Sheffield Challenge Cup by defeating Sheffield United. In 1896-97 and 1898-99, they were Champions of the Midland League and joined League Division II in 1901 but after a few seasons were not re-elected and were back in the Midland League. In 1915 Doncaster disbanded and a new company was not established until 1920. They moved to the Belle Vue ground in August 1922.

Only Time Cup Won By Non-League Club

Tottenham Hotspur still a Southern League team in 1901, defeated Sheffield United

There was often a motive, other than love of the game, for the foundation of clubs in the Victorian age, the desire to improve one's fellow men. Many clubs were connected in the early days with the church or chapel, often started by some young clergyman anxious to introduce the benefits of football to the men of his congregation and so divert them from less worthy pursuits!

On the other side of the coin, the public house was such a central feature of working-class life that it would have been strange if it had not played a major role in soccer's growth. Many teams whose origins lay elsewhere, used pubs as changing rooms - one of a range of services the pub supplied in this period.

The Lancashire textile area was to be a major early focus for working-class soccer. The importance of the Saturday half-day speeded up the process but towns where the half-day was delayed slowed the growth of the game. In Liverpool, a city with a high proportion of non-unionised casual workers, the game grew only slowly - similar factors may well have happened in London. While Birmingham newspapers recorded 811 matches in 1879-80, Liverpool noted only two - the Liverpool and District Football Association was not founded until 1882.

England's first seven internationals were all against Scotland, the Scots winning four, England one and two draws. The next new opponents were Wales in January 1879 at the Oval, England winning 2-1. The first game England v Ireland followed in 1882.

There have been several footballers who have played for England both at football and cricket, the first player being Hon. A. Lyttleton, Old Etonians forward and Middlesex batsman - capped for England v Scotland 1877 and 4 Tests v Australia 1880-84.

Manchester City's history can be traced back to 1880 in the Gorton area of the city. In 1865 St. Mark's Church opened in Clowes Street, West Gorton and working men's meetings set up by Anna Connell created St Mark's Cricket Club later in 1879. The following year, a football section was established, playing under the name of St. Mark's West Gorton or simply just West Gorton, but in 1881 they parted company from the host church - church officials objected to the team bringing in players from outside the local community to improve its performances.

The club merged with Gorton Athletic (founded 1884) to form Ardwick in 1887 and moved to Hyde Road, which was the team's first properly enclosed ground - staying there until the end of the 1922-23 season before Maine Road was built. In 1920 Hyde Road became the first provincial ground to be visited by a reigning monarch, when King George V visited - seven months later the main stand was destroyed by fire.

The first success for Ardwick was winning the Manchester Senior Cup in 1891 v Newton Heath (Manchester United) and joining the Football Alliance League. The Manchester Cup was won again the next season, this time by defeating Bolton Wanderers.

When the Second Division was started for 1892-93, Ardwick were elected as founder members - finishing 5th in their first season. In 1894 the club was reformed as Manchester City in a bid to create a team to represent Manchester.

This year, one of the most famous players of the era, Billy Meredith, came from the Welsh mining community

BILLY MEREDITH, Manchester United & City

and was working underground by the age of eleven. A right winger, he was signed from Chirk (Wales) after he had played six matches for Northwich Victoria and was later involved in a massive football scandal. He was suspended from 4th August 1905 to 30th April 1908 for having offered a sum of money to an Aston Villa player to let City win. The Villa player in evidence, said he took Meredith's proposal as a joke - Meredith stated that he acted on behalf of the secretary of the club.

The following March, another F. A. Commission looked at a charge that Meredith, while under suspension, had demanded his wages and had visited the dressing-rooms. He was put on the transfer list and signed by Manchester United for £500 even though his ban lasted another 18 months!

In 1921 he returned to City - between making his debut for City in November 1894 and his final appearance in a cup match in March 1924, Billy Meredith created a record having played in over a 1000 first class games and retired at the age of 49. His trademark was that in all the games he played, including Cup-Finals and Internationals, he was chewing a quill toothpick - there is no doubt that as a player he was a genius (see photo).

City finished top of Division II in 1898-99 and were the first club to be automatically promoted as the Test Match system had finished - runners up in their first season in the League were Glossop North End. Manchester City were the first Manchester team to win a major trophy, defeating Bolton Wanderers 1-0 in the Cup Final at Crystal Palace in 1904 (see photo).

Fulham can be traced back to 1880, when boys of St. Andrew's Sunday School, West Kensington started a team and played at the nearest available ground in Fulham. The club was originally called Fulham St. Andrew's until they turned professional in 1898 and joined the Southern League. Having won this League in 1906-07, Fulham were elected into League Division II and reached the Semi-Final of the Cup the same season but were thrashed 6-0 by Newcastle United.

Preston North End were formed in 1880, originally for cricket (1865) and Rugby but the winter sport turned to soccer in 1881. In 1885-86, the club played 65 matches with only two defeats and three draws - scoring 318 goals against 60. 'Proud Preston' as they were known, were one of the first crossing and heading teams and were to be the first club to achieve the 'double'. They won the League in the first season of 1888-89 without being defeated and won the Cup 3-0 v Wolverhampton with amateur goalkeeper Dr. Mills-Roberts. Preston were League Champions again the following season but not quite so easily, two points clear of Everton.

Another new club this season was **Ipswich Town**, although founded back in 1880, they did not become a professional club until as late as 1936. The Suffolk club eventually joined League Division III (South) for 1938-39 season. Their first honour was Champions of this league in 1953-54, finishing three points clear of Brighton - sadly Ipswich finished second bottom in Division II but were top again of Division III (South) in 1956-57 on goal difference from Torquay United - promotion to the First Division came in 1960-61.

The season 1880-81 was the moment when the referee was first mentioned in the Laws and his powers increased - Law 15 stated:

'By mutual consent of the competing clubs in matches a referee shall be appointed whose duty shall be to decide in all cases of dispute between its umpires. He shall also keep a record of the game and act as time-keeper and in the event of un-gentlemanly behaviour on the part of any of the contestants the offender or offenders shall be cautioned, and in the case of violent conduct the referee shall have power to rule the offending player or players out of play and order him or them off the

Only Known Photo Of An Oval Cup Final

In 1887, Bayliss (West Brom.) heads for goal and Warner (Aston Villa) saves - No goal nets and umpire standing by far goalpost

World's First Football Club

Founded in 1857, an early Sheffield F.C. team photo taken c. 1890

Goal-Mouth Action From A Match In 1891

The year when the referee with whistle & notebook was transferred from the touchline to inside the playing area. Courtesy of the F.A

Royal Arsenal Football Club

Pictured just 2 years after the club was formed, the team for 1888-89 season

First Club To Do The 'Double'

Preston North End team, who won the Cup and the first season of the League in 1888-89
Back row: Dr. R.H. Mills-Roberts, J. Graham, Major W. Sudell, R. Holmes, D. Russell, Sir W.E.M. Tomlinson, Rt. Hon. R.W. Hanbury, R. Howarth, G. Drummond Front row: S. Thomson, P. Dewhurst, J. Goodall, J. Ross, J.Gordan

Last F.A. Cup Final Played At Oval Cricket Ground

Programme from the match, March 1892 at the Kennington Oval

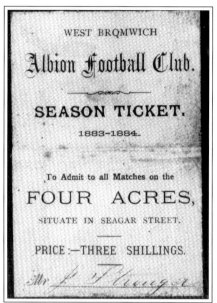

A season's football for 3s

Wolves Win F.A. Cup For First Time

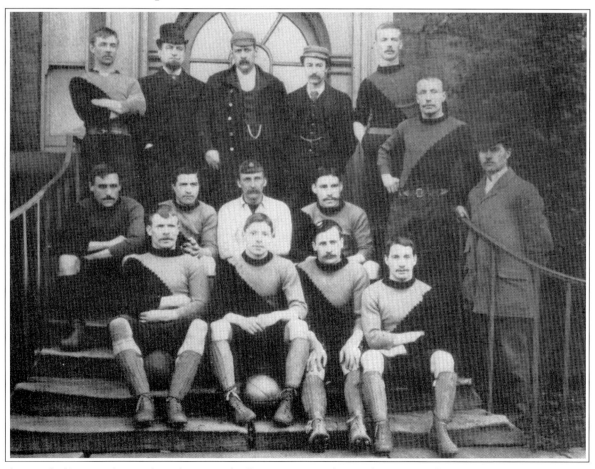

Photographed in 1893, players only; Back row: Baugh, Allen. Front row: Topham, Malpas, Rose, Swift, Kinsey.
Front row: Wykes, Butcher, Wood, Griffin

Original Accrington Football Club

Pictured in 1886 is the Accrington club - 2 years later, founder members of the Football League

ground, transmitting the name or names to the Committee of the Association under whose rules the game was played and in whom shall be solely vested the right of accepting an apology'

Even with this change, the referee's job was not easy, for the umpires could still be biased towards their own club and often disagreed on the occasion of a doubtful goal.

During this period there was now a rapid growth in new clubs - of those members of the Sheffield Association listed in the 1880 *Football Annual*, 16 were founded before 1870, while 34 started between 1870 and 1880. There was only one club affiliated to the Birmingham F.A. before 1870, nine had been founded between 1870 and 1875 and all 40 clubs joining the Lancashire F.A. had been founded in the previous ten years.

This season saw the last ever Cup Final between amateur clubs in the South, when the Old Carthusians beat the Old Etonians 3-0.

Burnley were founded in 1881. There was a Rugby club formed by members of the local Y.M.C.A. in the mid-1870s known as Burnley Rovers - it was mainly rugby played in and around Burnley at this time. The team merged with another local Association club in 1881, when a change was made to soccer, re-named Burnley and moved to Turf Moor. They were founder members of the Football League. In their second season Burnley did not win a game until March but stayed in the League. The first major success was winning the F.A. Cup in 1914 1-0 v Liverpool and becoming League Champions in 1920-21 season.

In 1881, the Lancashire Association had passed a rule banning the signing of Scottish players who were tempted South not only for football but also employment.

The following year, Accrington were expelled from the F. A., having been found guilty of an 'inducement' to attract a player from Church F.C. (near Accrington).

Swindon Town was formed in 1881 by the Rev. W. Pitt for young men of his parish. He was captain of an offshoot of a cricket club called the Spartans. In 1883, the club merged with St. Mark's Young Men's Friendly

Society and changed their name to Swindon Town - becoming professional in 1894. They were original members of the Southern League in 1894 and played on the Croft until 1896, when they moved to the County Ground. They competed in the Cup for the first time in 1907 and made it to the Semi-Final three years later, losing to Newcastle. Swindon won the Southern League in 1911 and again in 1914 and joined the new Third Division of the League in 1920.

Leyton Orient also came on the scene in 1881, starting out as Clapton Orient - the 'Orient' name was a suggestion from their player Jack Dearing. He worked for the Orient Steam Company and thought it would add some mystery to the club! Like most teams, an amateur organisation at first - going professional in 1901. Clapton joined Division II in 1905 and stayed in that division until dropping into Division III (South) in 1929. The club did not change its name until as late as 1946.

Season 1881-82 saw a new law passed by the F. A. - giving power to the umpires and referee to allow a goal when the ball had been handled by a player other than the goalkeeper, if in their opinion the ball would have passed between the posts - this rule only lasted for one season.

For 1881-82, a provincial club Blackburn Rovers reached the Final of the Cup for the first time - losing 1-0 to the Old Etonians at the Oval.

Tottenham Hotspur were formed in 1882. There existed the Hotspur Cricket Club, mostly comprising of boys attending Mr. Cameron's school and the Grammar School - it was decided to start a football club. The Casey brothers played a major part, providing the club's first goalposts, painted blue and white! There were 18 members at the end of the first year and the opening match with a club outside the district was against Homerton College.

The origin of the name Hotspur - at the original meeting one of the lads had been reading the history of England in the early fifteenth century and he was full of admiration for Henry Percy, nicknamed Hotspur, son of the Earl of Northumberland, who performed heroic deeds on the battle field. They first played on the Tottenham Marsh. Their first private ground was at North Park on which they played in 1888 - in summer months the pitch was let for tennis tournaments.

In 1899 Spurs entered the Southern League and won the F. A. Cup in 1901 defeating Sheffield United 3-1 in a replay at Bolton after a 2-2 draw - **since the Football League was formed, this the only time the Cup has been won by a non-League club.** (see photo)

Newcastle United can trace their history back to 1882 to a team called Newcastle West End and did not welcome new club Newcastle East End the following year, who took what little support was going. When Mr. Tom Watson took over control the West End club was struggling, the balance in the bank being nil! With the backing of William Neasham, he secured a 14 years' lease of a few acres of land which the club had the audacity, as some thought, to christen St. James' Park. The players' dressing-room was a small cabin, and the pitch left a lot to be desired! The two Newcastle clubs amalgamated under the name Newcastle West End and joined the Northern League in 1889.

The first match was not a financial success as the gate money amounted to 7s. 11d, Mrs. Watson, the only woman present was the most enthusiastic spectator and her optimistic outlook was her ability to turn St. James' Park into a 'going concern'.

In 1893 Newcastle West End joined League Division II. After a financial crisis the club became Newcastle United in 1895 and in season 1897-98 the First Division was reached. Newcastle became League Champions in 1904-05, 1906-7 and 1908-09 and F. A. Cup winners for the first time in 1910, beating Barnsley 2-0 at Everton after 1-1 in the first match at Crystal Palace.

Darlington were formed and first played as an amateur team in the Northern League, becoming professional in 1908 and joined the North-Eastern League. In 1918 they moved to join Darlington Cricket Club at the Feethams ground. Darlington were Champions of the North-Eastern League in 1920-21 and original members of Division III (North) the following season.

In Manchester by 1882, Association football was making slow progress - Rugby was almost exclusively played with clubs scattered around the area, whilst in East Lancashire the dribbling game had taken over.

Problems were raised by the importation of players and the paying of them by so called amateur clubs, Scotsmen were growing in numbers in the English game - finding gold coins in their pockets after a match! In 1882 the F. A. passed a rule stopping payment of any sort to players above their actual expenses 'and any wages actually lost by such players taking part in any match'. It was decided any players breaking this rule should be banned from the Cup and International matches and any club 'employing' such a player should be dropped from membership.

In this year the F. A. proposed there should be a meeting between the four national Associations of the United Kingdom to agree over the Laws of football. At first, the Scottish F. A. was reluctant to participate at such a

England v Scotland in 1893

Played at Richmond; Back row: W. McGregor, R.C. Gosling, J.J. Bentley, J. Holt, J.C. Clegg, G. Kinsey, R. Holmes, J. Goodall; Middle row: W.I. Bassett, J. Reynolds, G.H. Cotterill, L.H. Gay, A.H. Harrison; Front row: F. Spiksley, E. Chadwick

meeting - they preferred to retain their own version of the rules and did not want any interference with their independence. The English F. A. threatened to stop matches with Scotland and a serious break-down of negotiations seemed likely before the Scots relented and agreed to join the other home countries.

The meeting was held at Manchester, December 6th 1882 and was attended by two members of each of the four Associations - it was an immediate success. A combined code of rules was drawn up and agreed upon - the International Football Association Board was established.

The one-handed throw-in was further changed to now the two-handed throw, but the run up to the line was still permitted.

The F. A. brought in a new rule in 1882, which allowed for the payment of expenses to players, including broken time payments, for those involved in F. A. Cup ties.

There was a record win in the International Championship in February 1882, when England beat Ireland 13-0 in Belfast.

In 1882-83, the Cup went to the North for the very first time when Blackburn Olympic beat the Old Etonians 2-1 (see photo). The centre-half of Blackburn also coached the team and took them away to Blackpool. It was the first time proper training had been enforced. When the Cup was presented in front of the Oval pavilion to captain Warburton, the fans went mad with excitement - winning was more in their dreams than reality. Cheering, waving crowds and brass bands greeted their return to Lancashire - driven through the streets by wagonette drawn by six horses. It is interesting to note the occupations of the winning team: three weavers, a spinner, a cotton operative, an iron worker, a picture framer, a master plumber, a dentist's assistant and two others who were disguised professionals. The Blackburn club had been in existence for five years, but like many in this period soon went into oblivion.

The Cup was not to return to the place of its birth for nearly twenty years. Times had changed when a northern working-class club was able to enter what had been a pastime for gentlemen of leisure and beat them at their own game.

The good years of the Old Boys teams was now over. This was the last time one reached a Final but still appeared in the earlier rounds over the next few years and eventually faded into the background. The only exception were the Old Carthusians who reached the Semi-Final in 1884-85 season. Fewer and fewer middle-class and 'gentlemen' players appeared in first-class Association Football. **We should not forget what a major part the Universities and Public Schools played in the early development of the game of football.**

The F. A.'s income for many years was from subscriptions, for instance in 1875 a cash balance of only £2 17s. 5d. - in 1883 the rules gave all the gate-money of the semi-final and final of the Cup to the governing body, allowing it to build up a substantial reserve fund.

In the early rules, with club expenses almost non-existent and the game played by amateurs merely for fun, there was no reference to gate money. A clause was drafted in 1883 by N.C. Bailey which stated that receipts in all Cup-Ties be divided equally between the two clubs up to the Semi and Final - after paying the costs for the referee, umpires, police and third-class rail fares of the visiting players.

By 1883, the second centre-forward was removed to play in a new position, that of centre-half - combining both attack and defence. The first team to play this way was Cambridge University - it wasn't long before the advantages of the new formation were taken up by all clubs. The idea of five forwards, three half-backs, two backs and a goalkeeper had come to stay for a long time.

In February 1883, Cheshire played their 6th annual match v Staffordshire at the Macclesfield Ground - the Cheshire team consisted of five Macclesfield players, four from Northwich Victoria and two from the Crewe Alexandra club.

For the 1883-84 season the International Championships of the British Isles came into being, with Scotland as the first Champions.

Stockport County were formed in 1883 by members of Wycliffe Congregational Church, Wellington Road North at a meeting in McLaughlin's Café, Wellington Road South. In the summer of 1883, Messrs. Riley, Ashworth, Holden and Hewitt were playing cricket for the Wycliffe Sunday School team and their names also appear in the new football club called Heaton Norris Rovers - therefore we can assume these young men who were scholars at Stockport Sunday School, attended that original café get together.

The Rovers first played where No. 1 Spinning Mill is sited, then home of Heaton Norris Wanderers Cricket Club - soon moving to a field at Chorlton's Farm, Didsbury Road. Another club called Heaton Norris had started and played at the 'Ash Inn' ground on Manchester Road - they amalgamated with the Rovers in 1885-86 under the name Heaton Norris on the Ash. In 1887-88 the club moved to Wilkes Field, Belmont Street, then for 1890-91 went to play behind the 'Nursery Inn' at Green Lane where the players changed in an adjoining barn . The present name of Stockport County came in 1891, after the town was made a county borough.

England v Scotland at Sheffield

England centre-forward Woodward heads towards goal at Bramall Lane in 1903, Scotland won 2-1

County's first League was the Combination in 1891, Lancashire League in 1894 and they joined Division 11 in 1900. The following year was one of the most critical in the club's history, and in March, when the players had not been paid their wages for a week or two, there was almost a revolt! The players picked their own team and shared the gate money, receiving a sovereign each for two weeks' wages.

In 1902 the club moved to their present ground Edgeley Park, having to share for a short time with the rugby club who had been playing there since the 1880's. Stockport dropped out of the Second Division in 1904, but returned the following season and stayed in that League until 1921 and became the first champions of the new Division lll (North) in 1921-22.

Coventry City was founded in 1883 in a cycle factory by young men who came from the Birmingham district and their first name was Singers F. C. In 1891, their first award came when they won the Birmingham Junior Cup Final played at Perry Bar, Birmingham - Aston Villa's old ground. In 1894 they were elected to the Birmingham and District League, which included reserve teams such as Aston Villa, West Brom, Birmingham and Wolves. The name change to Coventry City came in 1898. In 1908, the club joined the Southern League and League Division II in 1919.

Bristol Rovers were founded in 1883 and originally known as the Black Arabs and wore black shirts with a sash of yellow ribbon. They soon beame Eastville Rovers until 1897-98 season, when the club joined the professional section of the Western League as Bristol Eastville Rovers - the following season their name changed to Bristol Rovers. For a number of years the Rovers' colours were hoops of light blue and white, when the grandfather of the Duke of Beaufort was President.

Bristol turned professional in 1897 and played in the Birmingham and Western Leagues, before moving up to the Southern League. They were Champions of the Southern League in 1904-05 and were founder members of Division III in 1920.

Lincoln City also started in 1883, playing in local and minor leagues before joining the Midland League. They played until 1894 at John o' Gaunt's ground prior to Sincil Bank. The club were Midland League Champions for the first time in 1889-90 and were original members of the Second Division in 1892. Lincoln were in and out of Division II three times before being part of the new Division III (North) in 1921. Their first season showed a heavy loss of £1,442 and no profit until 1926.

Tranmere Rovers were established in 1883 following the merger of Lyndhurst Wanderers and Belmont Cricket Club - under the presidency of James McGaul, Belmont F.C. were formed and won their first match v Brunswick Rovers 4-0 on November 15th 1884. Less than one year later the club changed its name to Tranmere Rovers, playing in blue shirts and white shorts at Steele's Field on Borough Road, Birkenhead.

By 1887, Rovers had moved to Ravenshaw's Field. The final switch was to their current ground at Prenton Park in 1912.

The club played in various minor competitions including the Liverpool and Wirral League. In 1899, a crisis occurred - when the committee divided and the larger number left Tranmere Rovers, taking the players with them and forming a new club Birkenhead F.C. Aldermen McGaul and Halsall plus messrs Mayor, Lees and Dawson remained loyal to the club. The new outfit of Birkenhead lasted only seven years before folding , but the record of the Rovers from that time onwards has been one of progress.

Tranmere entered the Lancashire Alliance, then the old Combination, followed by the Lancashire Combination. They moved up to the Central League in 1919 - after two successful seasons, the Rovers were elected to Football League Division 111 (North) for 1921-22 season.

William Ralph 'Dixie' Dean , one of the all time greatest goal scorers, started his League career at Tranmere. Whilst playing for village teams on the Wirral, he scored 18 goals in one day - six each in three different games! He signed amateur forms on 27th November 1923 and played his first game four days later for the Reserves' v Whitchurch at Prenton Park - scoring of course! In less than half a season, including a four week lay-off for a bad injury, he still led the Reserves' scoring list with 23 league and cup goals. He made his league debut at the age of just 16 years 355 days in 1924 - Dean scored 27 goals in 30 games for Tranmere, before being transferred across the River Mersey to Everton for £3,000.

On Boxing Day in 1935, Tranmere scored a record 13-4 win v Oldham Athletic - Robert 'Bunny' Bell entered the record books, when the striker scored an amazing nine goals and missed a penalty!

The club were in financial difficulties in 1979 after relegation to Division 1V - a £200,000 loan from Wirral Council helped secure Tranmere's survival. With debts mounting again by 1987, the club obtained an administration order through the courts - local businessman Peter Johnson took control and ownership of Rovers.

The vigorous new clubs of the North took the place of the Old Boys' teams. It was the other Blackburn team the Rovers who now went on to win three years running 1884-5-6 as the Wanderers had done nearly ten years earlier.

In an attempt to maintain the high standard of amateur football and to achieve something like the Wanderers, a team known as the Corinthians was started in 1883.

One of its rules stopped it from entering any competitions, but in its early years the club would have done well in the F. A. Cup if they had entered.

During the reign of the Old Boys' teams spectators were limited and even at the Cup Final there were never more than 5,000 for the first eight years. As the origin of the players changed and the game moved north, the crowds began to rapidly increase.

In both the 1884 and 1885 finals, Blackburn Rovers faced the same opponents - Queen's Park, Glasgow - winning 2-1 and 2-0 (see photo). The side from North of the border at this time was full of internationals and virtually represented Scotland, making the Finals into more of an international contest - the three previous matches between the clubs had all ended in draws. In the Blackburn ranks was the once mysterious Fergie Suter who had taken part in those earlier and famous matches for Darwen v the Old Etonians - he was now

one of the ever increasing number of unauthorised professionals. Amongst the record crowd of 12,000 who watched the first encounter at the Oval, were Blackburn fans who released scores of pigeons as the teams took to the field - the competition this season had attracted the record number of 101 clubs.

In the Semi-Final of 1884-85, when Queen's Park drew with Notts Forest at Derby, the F. A. directed the replay to be held at Merchiston Castle Ground, Edinburgh - the only time a Semi-Final has been played out of England.

It had become usual for crowds of fans to watch their teams for away matches, the system of railway excursions had made this possible - apart from problems at the actual game, their invasion of the town before and after was not always welcomed by the local public. When thousands of Blackburn supporters travelled to London in 1884 for the first all-northern Final, they were referred to by the *Pall Mall Gazette* as 'a northern horde of uncouth garb and strange oaths', whose activities were like a tribe of Sudanese Arabs let loose! The 'uncouth garb' referred to the new craze for fans to wear hats, caps, scarves and umbrellas in club colours - sometimes in fancy dress complete with musical instruments, bells and rattles, in order to attract attention and make their presence felt.

Bury Win F.A. Cup by Record Score

The Bury team which defeated Derby County 6-0 in 1903 - Back row: W. Johnstone, J. Lindsay, F. Thorpe, H. Monteith, G.W. Ross (Captain), J. McEwan; Front row: W. Richards, W. Wood, C. Sagar, J. Leeming, J. Plant.

Southampton's First Match at the Dell

September 1898, opening match v Brighton United - semi-circular markings for goal area.

As in previous centuries, football was regarded by some as a social evil due to the drunkenness and fighting after matches - at least the game was not played in the streets like days of old!

Inside the grounds, the crowds of the 1880s must have been fairly well-behaved, police coverage was nothing like as thorough as today.

Leicester City were founded in 1884 as Leicester Fosse by old boys of Wyggeston School, most of whom lived near to the old Roman Fosse (fort). The young men had a whip-round of 9d. each for the purchase of a ball and with the help of a carpenter made a rough set of goalposts, the cost covered by a further 9d. fee - at the end of the first season, the balance in hand was 1s. 10d. In 1888, their Belgrave Road ground was taken over by Leicester Rugby Club and a move was made to Victoria Park. They joined the Midland League in 1890 and League Division II in 1894 and changed their name to Leicester City in 1919.

Derby County started in the spring of 1884, a William Morley was the main person who brought the club to life. The town had a football tradition and the Derbyshire Cricket Club, in whose interests Derby County was formed, agreed to the provision of an ideal playing area on the county ground. At first, chocolate, amber and blue were the colours for both football and cricket. The first playing member was Haydn Morley and the first match v Great Lever (near Bolton), of 34 games played in the first season, 14 were won. When they joined the League as founder members in 1888, their ground was Pike's Lane, a move to the Baseball Ground was made in 1895.

Chester City were formed in 1884. One of the cricket clubs was called Chester Rovers who played on the Roodee (site of Chester Racecourse) - by 1880, a football section was started by members of local football teams Chester Wanderers and St. Oswalds. Chester Rovers emerged as one of the main clubs in Chester, alongside St. Oswalds and Chester College - a crowd of 300 watched a game in March 1883 v Trinity Ramblers.

Members of King's School, who had helped in the growth of football in the area, had formed Old King's Scholars team - making the Semi-Final of the Cheshire Cup in 1882-83, beaten by Northwich Victoria, who had won the cup since its start in 1879-80.

Towards the end of 1883-84 season, an attempt was made to form a more representative club which could challenge the supremacy of Northwich Victoria and Crewe Alexandra in Cheshire - trial matches were held with players picked from the area to create a team called Chester Football Association - short lived organisation!

For the start of the 1884-85 Chester Rovers moved to a new ground at Faulkner Street in the Hoole area of the City - this ground was rented from the Earl of Kilmorey by the Weaver Brothers (coach and cab makers) in Flookersbrook - known as Weaver's Field. The club played friendly matches against clubs from the Chester, North Wales and Liverpool areas and struggled financially. It was decided that three of the best players from the Old King's Scholars team would join the Chester Rovers on a permanent basis.

For the following season the name of the club changed to Chester F. C. with changes to the committee and people who were involved in the Chester Association project earlier, now becoming the premier club in the City, taking over from Chester St. Johns and Chester St. Oswalds - the other clubs were not amused the name of Chester had been adopted!

The Chester club used the 'Ermine Hotel' on Hoole Road as a dressing-room and the first game was lost at Earlestown in September 1885 - the first home game at Faulkner Street v Northwich Victoria attracted 800 fans, losing 3-0. The club were beaten in both the Welsh and Cheshire Cups, the latter defeat v a 'third rate' Middlewich team in a brutal game in which several players were badly injured!

Organising any friendly matches of this period was a hit and miss affair. Chester were no exception, as teams from Liverpool failed to turn up and Bootle arrived so late it was finished in darkness! Chester was also at fault v Hartford St. Johns - catching a 4pm train for a 3.30pm kick off!

There were often disputes with the referee and umpires. In a game v Chirk, the ex-Chirk player who was the referee was determined the Welsh side would not lose - the Chester umpire and players called the referee a 'rogue' and walked off! In 1888-89 an F. A. Cup Qualifying match v Macclesfield at home ended 2-2, with extra-time scheduled. The Macclesfield team left the field, stating they had a train to catch - with no

opposition Chester kicked off and simply walked the ball through the goal to win 3-2!

Chester's early successes were winning the Cheshire Senior Cup in 1895, 1897 and 1904 - later were champions of the Cheshire County League in 1922, 1926 and 1927. The club joined the Football League Division 3 (North) for season 1931-32, when the accounts showed a profit on the previous season of £2,250 6s. 1d. - the gate receipts were £8,165 4s. 4d. and wages to players and trainers being £2,329 17s. 4d.

Rotherham United started in 1884. A few football fans in the Thornhill area got together near a gas lamp in one of the public streets and agreed to form a club known as Thornhill United. A playing area was found adjoining the Red House Inn, but the ground had a large slope and was too small for F.A. Cup games.

In 1905-6 season the club was re-named as Rotherham County and joined the Midland League. Having merged with Rotherham Town in 1925, the present name of Rotherahm United was finally adopted.

Blackburn's third Cup win on the run was 2-0 v West Bromwich Albion - this followed a 0-0 draw in the initial match - the Midlands team had watched the boat race, became chilled, rushed lunch and only just had time to reach the Oval! For the first time in the Cup's history, the replay was played outside of London at Derby County cricket ground - heavy snow fell in the morning but 12,000 still turned up.

In recognition of their three wins in a row, Blackburn were presented by the F. A. with a silver shield.

Betting on matches was taking place, as it was on other sports like the Oxford v Cambridge boat race - a bad example had been set by the 'gentleman' of the period!

During the 'Blackburn years', there were important issues taking place in the background - the question of the player who was supposed to be an amateur on the surface at least, but was in fact being paid for his services.

In the 1870s and 1880s, 'professionalism' had covered a number of 'offensive practices' including paying above the rates for broken time work, hiring players for certain matches and offering many inducements relating to off the field activities - the provision of employment opportunities. Such activities were clearly common in Lancashire from 1882-83, judging by the flood of leading Scottish players into the county's best clubs. By 1883, Burnley could field a team with ten Scotsmen and Preston regularly fielded nine in the 1884-85 season. Local talent was also poached from rival clubs, Preston

Liverpool v Burnley 1914, views of both ends of the ground

Newcastle Team in F.A. Cup Final

Pictured in 1905 before the game v Aston Villa, Newcastle lost 2-0

Action from 1905 Cup Final

Hampton scoring one of his two goals for Aston Villa v Newcastle United - good viewing from the trees!

luring a George Wilson from Blackburn Olympic by offering him the tenancy of the Black-a-Moor-Head public house.

There were several possible methods used to make payment possible by clubs, duplicate sets of books were often kept - one out of the way and one for viewing by the F. A. Players were given bogus jobs for which they received payment, the money being refunded to the 'employers' by the clubs. Another scheme was to pay the players out of the gate money before the total was entered in the books as gross receipts.

The Football Association, backed by the Associations of Birmingham and Sheffield wanted to keep the game amateur and kill off this 'offensive' practice. There were some investigations carried out, looking at the more obvious incidents from matches and some offenders were punished - the first club in late 1883 to be dealt with were Accrington, who were banned from the Cup after their 3-2 win v Park Road in an early round for paying one of their players.

Given more publicity, on January 19th 1884 - Preston North End drew 1-1 with London side Upton Park in the 4th round of the Cup - the Upton Park team immediately protested after the game about some of the players in

Last Cup Final at Stamford Bridge

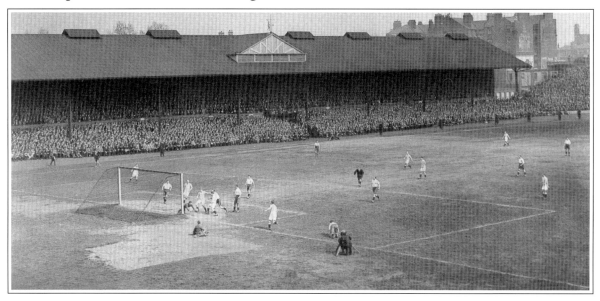

Huddersfield beat Preston 1-0 in 1922, before a move to Wembley.

the Preston team. When the enquiry took place by the F. A., Major Sudell, who had wanted to build a great team to oppose Blackburn, openly admitted that the club imported players to Preston and found them work. He argued that this was common amongst other Northern clubs and did not breach regulations. The F. A. still expelled North End from the competition - Burnley and Great Lever followed the same route by the beginning of next season.

It was inevitable that there would be an aggressive response and at the end of October a group of 31 leading clubs including not only most of the Lancashire clubs but also Aston Villa, Walsall Swifts and Sunderland, threatened to break-away from the F. A.

Certain members of the F. A. felt nothing could be done to stamp out the paid player - it was proposed to go this way but at the first meeting the decision was thrown out due to the strong opposition from the Sheffield and Birmingham Associations led by J. C. Clegg and C. Crump. In June 1884, the F. A. added that payments for lost wages should not apply to more than one day a week and banned any imported player or any but Englishmen to play with English clubs in the Cup.

It took until 29th July 1885 before a Special General Meeting was set up at Auderton's Hotel, Fleet Street, London - considering the importance of the subject of professionalism, the turn out surprisingly only numbered 50 members instead of the usual 200. By 35 votes to 15, the necessary two-thirds majority carried in favour of paid players.

The F. A. realised for some time they were facing a losing battle and agreed that 'it is now expedient in the interests of Association Football, to legalise the employment of professional football players, but only under certain restrictions'. Clubs were allowed to pay players provided they were either born or had lived for two years within a six-mile radius of the ground - in addition professionals had to be registered annually. Any player who accepted money other than travelling or hotel expenses would be regarded as a professional - no professional was allowed to play for more than one club in the same season without special permission.

In the early 1880s, leading players were in a strong bargaining position, able to move clubs when they wished by usually illegal methods - as a result of the F. A. meeting, the players had lost some of their power. The whole idea was still viewed in the South with horror. It was not until 1891 that Arsenal were the first London club to go professional .

Payment had been made to cricket players for several years, so it was a natural progression for football to go the same way, but the F. A. were quick to ensure that the legalised professional knew his place. Professionals and ex-professionals were effectively prevented from being allowed to shape the game's development as they were banned from sitting on F. A. committees. In 1885, despite the new ruling, the Sheffield F. A. initially opposed professionalism amongst its members and for a while some bitterness remained - soon the growing football family was to be united again.

In Rugby Union, the middle-class attitude still won through and a proposal to have professionalism in the game was defeated - there were fewer working-class players of Rugby than soccer.

1911 Cup Final at Old Trafford

Bradford City 1-0 winners v Newcastle United, the ground was opened the previous year.

Aerial view of the first Cup Final at Wembley in 1923 - the crowd invaded the pitch

The first professional player to play for England in 1885 was the Blackburn half-back Forrest at the age of nineteen v Scotland, he played in a blue shirt with his amateur colleagues in their standard white strip. The Scottish authorities objected to his selection, stating that both teams should be strictly amateur but there was nothing in the rules of the International Board to support this view.

The other home countries continued to wage war against 'this evil' of professionalism, but all in turn had to submit to the inevitable - Scotland finally lifting their ban in May 1893.

The A.G.M. of the Cheshire F.A. took place in June 1885. The number of clubs who were now members had grown from 8 to 16 over the previous year.

Southampton were formed in 1885 by some youths of St. Mary's, the parish church of Southampton Young Men's Association conceiving the idea of a football club and asked Archdeacon Wilberforce to be their first President. In 1887, they won the Hampshire Junior Cup and for each year until 1890, when they claimed the trophy as their own property.

Application to join the Southern League in 1895 was refused but accepted when a club dropped out - Southampton broke all records winning the Championship unbeaten! Their connection with the church lasted until 1897, when the name of St. Mary's changed to Southampton and they moved to the Dell in 1898 (see photo). They were F. A. Cup finalists in 1900 and 1902, losing to Bury and Sheffield United.

Queen's Park Rangers were founded in 1885 by Jack McDonald and Fred Weller with the help of the Rev. Gordon Young who formed a team from some boys at Droop Street Board School, Queen's Park. This became attached to St. Jude's Institute, whose name the club adopted. Such was the state of their finances, that club's gear, consisting of four upright posts and two pieces of tape, had to be carried to their pitch at Welfords Fields. The club went professional in 1898, when it changed to Queen's Park Rangers.

Another London club, **Millwall** started in 1885, by employees of Morton & Co. - a jam and marmalade factory in West Ferry Road and formed a team under the name of Millwall Rovers. The first ground was in Glengall Road, and the next year was a private enclosure at the rear of the 'Lord Nelson'. In 1887 the club became joint holders of the East End Cup. In the following two seasons, Millwall again won this trophy, which became their own property. In 1890, another ground move - a lease taken on the East Ferry Road pitch.

Two years later, Millwall won two cups, the Luton and District Charity and the Middlesex Junior. They were founder members of the Southern League when it begun in 1894, winning the championship by gaining 28 points out of a possible 32. In season 1899-1900, the club reached the semi-final of the F. A. Cup, losing 3-0 to Southampton after a 0-0 draw.

Luton Town was formed by the merger of Luton Wanderers and Luton Excelsior clubs - the Wanderers claim to earlier fame was a draw with the famous Old Etonians in a Cup match. Luton Town is the oldest professional club in the South of England - in 1890 an offer of 5s. per week was made to each of three local players. At the end of the season, it was decided to pay the whole team - 2s 6d. per week with an extra 6d. for away matches plus payment for working time lost before 12 noon on Saturdays. The club joined Division II in 1897, but failed to gain re-election in 1900 and were back in the Southern League until Division III was formed in 1920.

Bury started following a public meeting held in 1885 at the 'Waggon and Horses Hotel', attended largely by members of Bury Wesleyans and Unitarians football clubs, who had been attracted to the sport from seeing games in Sheffield and Bolton. The club was officially formed at a subsequent gathering at the 'Old White Horse Hotel', Fleet Street on 24th April 1885. Bury became sub-tenants of a field on one of the Earl of Derby's farms and have been here ever since at Gigg Lane. The first match was an exhibition game in June 1885, gate receipts were £11 9s. Bury were responsible for the formation of the Lancashire League in 1889 and were champions in 1890-91. They followed this by winning the Lancashire Senior Cup the following season, the first the club had entered.

The nickname 'The Shakers', came in a moment of enthusiasm from the chairman J.T. Ingham, who said 'We'll give them a shaking; in fact we are the Shakers'. The club were elected into Division II in 1894 and were champions in their first season. In 1900 Bury won the F. A. Cup 4-0 v Southampton but created a record Cup Final score 6-0 v Derby County in 1903 (see photo). Like Preston had achieved in 1889, Bury won the Cup without conceding a goal.

The majority of public school footballers of the 1860s were sportsmanlike, although a time when doubt and disagreement on the field of play were common, owing to the fact that the rules were in a state of change, the 'gentlemen' players mainly behaved like gentlemen. They sought no unfair advantage, treated their opponents with respect and when an agreement was made stuck to it. A great deal of this was lost during those next 30 years - can we put this down to professionalism? There

Cup Finals Come To Stamford Bridge

Aston Villa collect the Cup in 1920 after defeating Huddersfield Town 1-0, the first of three finals held at Chelsea's ground

First Wembley F.A. Cup Final

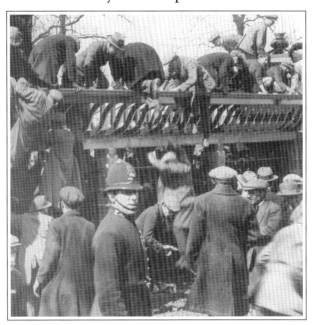

Fans storm the turnstiles in 1923, when Bolton Wanderers played West Ham

were many arguments on the subject but the numerous changes to the game in this period, were bound to make a big difference to the way players would play the game.

At Eton, football developed a more 'Association style', very little 'handling' allowed. The goals were 11x 7 feet, pitch of no fixed size, usually used a referee and featured 11 players a side (see photo). In 1860, an annual cup was introduced for the best house in the school. As far back as 1859, there were 49 recorded matches at this public school.

Harrow football allowed for a limited amount of 'handling'. The pitch was 150 x 100 yards in size, the goal was 12 feet wide but no height restriction and a referee also featured at this public school. Teams consisted of 12 players (see photo) for a few years, with no goalkeeper.

The first representative game between 'Gentlemen' and Players (professionals) took place at Preston in January 1886. The amateurs won 1-0. In the return match at Kennington Oval, the players included six Scots from English clubs, while the 'Gentlemen' were made up entirely of members of the Corinthian club - the professionals won 2-1 with the Prince of Wales (later King Edward VII) in attendance. These teams met 14 times, professionals winning nine, the amateurs three and two drawn.

England 'caps' were first introduced in 1886, when at a committee meeting of the F. A., a proposal made by N.L. Jackson was: 'That all players taking part for England in future international matches be presented

with a white silk cap with red rose embroidered on the front. These to be termed 'international caps' - the sub-committee later decided on a suitable cap, chose royal blue velvet and not white.

Davenham is a small picturesque village in Cheshire, yet in 1885-86 amazingly reached the last 16 of the F. A. Cup - their story could in some way apply to other villages in the early days of the Competition. Davenham F.C. was formed following a meeting at the Davenham National Schools in October 1879. A field lent by a Mr. Percival near the centre of the village, would be their pitch and the first captain Lea Jones. Officials and a committee were appointed and a subscription of 2/6d (12p) a year for seniors and juniors 1/6d (8p).

The man behind the success of the club was Matthew Earlam, who joined the club in 1880 first as player and captain, then as coach. Having learnt his Association football at York College in the early 70's, he played for Northwich Victoria and later became headmaster of Davenham National Schools. Earlier his leadership skills had already been recognised as he was captain of the first ever Cheshire representative team v Staffordshire in 1878 - two years later he was victorious captain of Northwich Victoria for the first Cheshire Cup Final v Hartford St. John's.

Earlam placed great emphasis on physical fitness and tactical skills - after a training session, the Davenham team, all born within a two mile radius, would meet in one of the classrooms in the school, where he would reveal his plans for the next match with diagrams chalked on the blackboard. This type of organisation was almost unheard for this period, but Earlam transformed the village team into one of the leading amateur clubs in the north of England.

Between 1885-87, Davenham reached three consecutive Cheshire Finals - winning in 1886 2-1 v Crewe Alexandra. This was a great achievement when you consider established clubs like Crewe, Macclesfield, Chester and Northwich Victoria were taking part. As Cup holders, Davenham played a challenge match v the F. A. Cup winners and professionals of Blackburn Rovers at Hartford Cricket Club - losing only 3-0.

Davenham's greatest performance in the same season was reaching the 5th round of the F. A. Cup - Round One: Golden Hill (Staffordshire) 2-1, Round Two: Macclesfield 8-1, Round Three: Crewe Alexandra 2-1, Round Four: Bye, Round Five: Lost 2-1 away at Small Heath Alliance (later Birmingham City), which was no disgrace as the Midlands outfit reached the Semi-Final.

The Davenham club merged in 1889 with Hartford St.John's to form Hartford and Davenham United and a year later joined up with Northwich Victoria.

Arsenal was started in 1886 by young men from the Midlands and the North, who were employed at the Royal Arsenal, Woolwich. The first name of the club was Dial Square, after the name of part of the Royal Arsenal armament factory. After a meeting at the 'Royal Oak' pub, this quickly changed to Royal Arsenal (see photo). Their first strip was red jerseys borrowed from Nottingham Forest with two military wagons as a grandstand! In the clubs' first season, just ten matches were played, 7 won, 1 drawn and 2 lost - for the following season a private ground was secured.

Following a meeting at the 'Windsor Castle Hotel', it was decided that the club should go professional for 1891-92 and change their name to Woolwich Arsenal. Most Southern clubs cancelled their fixtures with the Arsenal and they had to look to the Midland and Northern clubs for matches! A limited liability company with a capital of £4,000 was formed in 1893 and moved to the Manor Ground, which was their home for many years. The next important event was joining Division II for the 1893-94 season.

Plymouth Argyle's history goes back to 1886. The club was formed at a meeting in September, held in a room above the 'Borough Arms Coffee House', Bedford Street by former public and private school pupils. Devon was a popular area for Rugby and the club did much to popularise the Association game in the county. They were reorganised in 1903, when Plymouth became a professional club joining the Southern League and were Champions in 1913. Like many other clubs Plymouth

stayed in the Southern League until Division III was started in 1920. Chairman, A.C. Ballard was the first to offer an aeroplane for the team's away matches - turned down by the League committee!

Shrewsbury Town were formed this year and their first success was winning the Welsh Cup in 1891 and 1938. Their first player to play for Wales was J. Bowdler in 1889. They were Midland League Champions in 1937-38 and 1947-48. Shrewsbury is one of the newer additions to the Football League, not joining Division III (North) until 1950 but transferred to Division III (South) for the following season.

Back to the F. A. Cup in season 1886-87, Glasgow Rangers reached the Semi-Final and it was the last occasion any Scottish clubs entered the Competition. From the start, any clubs in the U.K. were given membership by the F. A., which was their qualification for entering the Cup - now the Scottish F. A. banned clubs under its control from competing for any other national trophy.

The following season, Preston created a record Cup score beating Hyde 26-0, not surprisingly still a record today - every player except the goalkeeper scored! Preston reached the final and it was the first time a ground was closed after 17,000 entered - Preston asked Major Marindin (Referee) if they could be photographed with the cup before the match, his reply: 'Had you not better win it first?' In fact they lost 2-1 to West Brom, a team of local players with a wage bill of less than £10 a week.

One of the earliest crowd problems came in January 1887, when Aston Villa toured Scotland. They were playing Queen's Park at Hampden Park, against a strong snowstorm scoring five goals and routing the powerful Scots. When the snow got worse, Queen's Park refused to come out after half-time - the match was abandoned. Feeling they had not received value for money, the fans proceeded to tear down what property they could, including the goalposts!

Barnsley were founded in 1887 by the Rev. Tiverton Preedy, curate of St. Peter's Church. Games played on the fields next to the church caused the problem of the footballs breaking the vicar's stained glass windows - the breakages earned them the title 'Little Tykes'. They first rented the Oakwell Ground from an Arthur Senior, playing local and friendly matches in the first year. In 1888 St. Peter's F.C. joined the Sheffield and Hallamshire Cup competition and became members of the Sheffield and District League in 1891. In 1893 the 'Saints' won the Barnsley Association Cup v Mexborough played at the Queen's Grounds after a replay. Gate receipts at Barnsley were £111.

In 1898 Barnsley St. Peter's joined League Division II and the following season changed their name to Barnsley, also their colours from blue and white to red. In 1910 Barnsley reached the F. A. Cup Final v Newcastle, after 1-1 at Crystal Palace lost the reply 2-0 at Everton.

Blackpool started on July 26th 1887 as Blackpool St. John's. It was created by members of the St. John's School, at meeting at the 'Stanley Arms Hotel', with the object to form a club bearing the town's name. The team in their first season, played at Raikes Hall Gardens. They joined the Lancashire League in 1890 and were elected to Division II in 1896-97, but back in the Lancashire League in 1899. Blackpool amalgamated with the South Shore club on December 12th 1899 and, much stronger, returned to the Second Division - South Shore were a successful club for many years, reaching the 6th round of the F. A. Cup in 1885-86. Blackpool's finest hour came in 1953, winning the F. A. Cup 4-3 v Bolton Wanderers - Stanley Matthews finally with a winner's medal.

Cheltenham Town can trace their history back to 1887 when an Albert White returned to his native town from College in London to introduce football to Cheltenham. Trials were held at the East Gloustershire Cricket Ground and the club was born. They played in local football for 30 years at three grounds - Agg-Gardner's Recreation Ground, Whaddon Road and Carter's Field. In 1932, Cheltenham changed to their red and white shirts and moved to the current ground at Whaddon Road - also turning professional. Entry to the Football League was finally gained in season 1999-2000.

Wycombe Wanderers were started in 1887 by a group of furniture-makers, following a meeting at the 'Steam Engine' public house. It is thought they were named after the famous F.A. Cup winners The Wanderers, who visited the town in 1877. After various grounds, the club settled at Loakes Park in High Wycombe in 1895. From 1896 the club played in the Southern League but struggled against professional teams, changing first to the Great Western and then the Spartan League. Having won the Spartan League in 1921, they joined the Isthmian League and the F. A. Amateur Cup was won in 1931. It would be 1956, before Wycombe won the first of eight Isthmian League titles. They were promoted to the Conference in 1990, and moved to Adams Park. Wycombe appointed Martin O'Neill as manager and were promoted to Division II in 1993.

Brentford were formed in 1888 with a starting membership of only twenty enthusiasts - the first captain was a J.J.K. Curtis. Their first ground was at Boston Park until 1904, when a move was made to Griffin Park. The first league they played in was the West London Alliance and they won the championship in 1893 plus the West Middlesex Junior and Senior Cups. They became one of the best amateur teams in London, in 1898 beating Ilford in the London Senior Cup. In 1900 the club decided to go professional and joined the Second Division of the Southern League - they were elected to League Division 111 in 1920.

Barnet F.C. were founded in 1888, having formerly been known as New Barnet (1885-88) and Woodville F.C. (1882-85). The club played in New Barnet before moving to Queens Road in 1889 and became members of the North London League in 1892-93. The club played in the North Middlesex and then the London League. The club was reformed in 1904 and stayed an amateur club and first played at the current Underhill Ground in 1907. Following another merger, Barnet reformed again in 1919 and competed in the Athenian League for over 50 years - joining the Football League in 1991.

The entries for the F. A. Cup had grown to 149, most employed professional players and there was a clear difference between the strengths of so many clubs. A R.P. Gregson came up with the idea of a qualifying competition - his idea was to divide the country into ten divisions to be managed in the early stages by District Committees. This scheme was accepted for season 1888-89 - the Cup was divided into two sections, a Qualifying and Competition Proper.

For this season, the rules were amended for gate money - half of the net proceeds from the Semi-Finals to be shared equally between the four clubs, the F. A. taking the other half and all the gate for the Final.

One of the consequences of professionalism was that clubs soon lost their local character, an eleven representing Birmingham might consist entirely of men from different parts of the country - a situation frowned upon by early amateur players. Football fans did not care where a man came from, as long as he played well for his club and building up a team which could triumph over local rivals was appealing!

By the late 1880s there were numerous professional teams. Now that clubs had a weekly wage bill and other expenses, they had to be sure of a weekly match - this was an uncertain factor. A friendly fixture could be cancelled at the last minute for various reasons, travel problems, one of the sides might have been involved in a Cup match - clubs knocked out in the early rounds could be left with vacant dates and no gate money. Matches were even cancelled as one team was unable to field a team for a particular game or the players wanted to watch another club play!

The answer which started solving the problem for clubs was found in 1888 by William McGregor, a Birmingham based Scotsman and draper by profession - a committee member of Aston Villa. The basic idea of a league followed one used in American Baseball and the idea was put forward by W.H. Mounsey of Manchester in the columns of *The Athletic News*.

McGregor's first move on 2nd March 1888 was to send a circular to 10 or 12 of the principal clubs suggesting they should combine playing home and away matches during the season. A meeting was held in London on the eve of the Cup Final, at which it was decided the Football League should be formed - the first name suggested by McGregor was The Association Football Union.

He persuaded twelve of the leading clubs, six from Lancashire and six from the Midlands, to enter an agreement to play each other regularly to a fixed programme - always fielding their strongest sides - enjoying an equal status to the F. A. but whose rules it observed.

The first AGM was at 'The Royal Hotel', Manchester on 17th April. Mr. McGregor was appointed President and Henry Lockett of Stoke, the Secretary. Rules were framed and adopted and the twelve clubs who formed the League agreed to an annual subscription of £2 2s. Other clubs, Sheffield Wednesday, Nottingham Forest, Halliwell (near Bolton) and amateur club Old Carthusians also applied but were not accepted. In Sheffield the proposal for the League was met with comments that the scheme would prove too costly, hence the absence of the Wednesday club from the original organisation.

The first five games were played on 8th September with a few early problems - Accrington arrived an hour late for their first match at Everton, while Stoke reached Preston's ground in October with only nine players - one having missed the train and another signed for a new club on the journey!

The system of two points for a win and one for a draw was not settled until after the season had started, there was strong opposition from those led by Mr. Louis Ford of West Brom who wanted drawn games ignored and points only awarded for victories.

This new scheme had an immediate effect, the clubs were sure of a steady income and the game itself improved as teams were playing good matches weekly. In view of this there was a huge increase in the number of fans wanting to see important matches in the following years - League games were soon having 10,000 or 20,000 every other week. Not surprisingly, the League idea caught on and over the next decade the League system spread throughout the country - both on a regional and local level.

EARLY PITCH MARKINGS FROM 1901

Brown has scored for Spurs v Sheffield United at Crystal Palace F.A. Cup Final

This was to be Preston's season. They played their first League match on September 8th and their last on January 5th - 22 games only, remaining unbeaten to win the first League by 11 points:-

		P	W	D	L	G	P
1	Preston North End	2	18	4	0	74-15	40
2	Aston Villa	22	12	5	5	61-43	29
3	Wolverhampton Wanderers	22	12	4	6	50-37	28
4	Blackburn Rovers	22	10	6	6	66-45	26
5	Bolton Wanderers	22	10	2	10	63-59	22
6	West Bromwich Albion	22	10	2	10	40-46	22
7	Accrington	22	6	8	8	48-48	20
8	Everton	22	9	2	11	35-46	20
9	Burnley	22	7	3	12	42-62	17
10	Derby County	22	7	2	13	41-60	16
11	Notts County	22	5	2	15	39-73	12
12	Stoke City	22	4	4	14	26-51	12

The 'double' was completed by Preston (see photo) when they defeated West Brom in the F. A. Cup 3-0. Preston did not concede a goal in the whole competition. There was a record crowd at the Oval of 22,000 with a further 2,000 turned away. It was so chaotic that one of the umpires Lord Kinnaird could not get into the ground - after a struggle, forced his way into the enclosure and reached the pavilion as the teams were taking the field!

The fee for referees for this first season of the League was 10/6d per match, linesmen were paid 5/-d in 1896 and increased to 1 guinea a year later for the referees.

The same time as the Football League started, there was a new Second Combination League, which due to poor organisation, lasted only one season.

Another attempt at a floodlit game took place at Belle Vue Gardens, Manchester, February 26th 1889. The match between Ardwick and Newton Heath was in aid of the Hyde Colliery Explosion Fund - a profit of £140 being raised. The illumination was not supplied by electricity, but by Wells lights - naphtha flares with air pressure forcing the oil to the burners.

Sheffield United were founded in 1889, one of its founder members being Sir Charles Clegg. Bramall Lane had opened as a cricket ground in 1855. It was one of the venues used by Yorkshire for many years and later various local clubs played football there. Sheffield F.C. was closely involved with the start of United, providing players for some of their early games and used to join in practice sessions with the professionals.

Sheffield United were elected into new League Division II in 1892 and by defeating Accrington in a 'Test' match

were promoted into Division I for the following season - after only nine years in existence were League Champions in 1898. This was United's finest period, winning the F. A. Cup in 1899 v Derby County 4-1 - after four matches v Liverpool in the Semi-Final. Finalists in 1901 and winners again in 1902, 1915 and 1925.

The second season of the League saw the setting up of a management committee and the introduction of goal average as the deciding factor when points were equal.

Season 1889-90 was the beginning of the important Football Alliance, which was to become Division II in 1892. Also starting now were the Northern and Midland Counties Leagues.

The first season of the Football Alliance ended as follows:-

		P	W	D	L	G	P
1	Sheffield Wednesday	22	15	2	5	70-39	32
2	Bootle	22	13	2	7	66-39	28
3	Sunderland Albion	22	12	2	8	67-44	28
4	Grimsby Town	22	12	2	8	58-47	26
5	Crewe Alexandra	22	11	2	9	68-59	24
6	Darwen	22	10	2	10	70-75	22
7	Birmingham St. George's	22	10	3	9	67-52	21
8	Newton Heath	22	9	2	11	40-44	20
9	Walsall Town Swifts	22	8	3	11	44-59	19
10	Small Heath	22	6	5	11	44-67	17
11	Nottingham Forest	22	6	5	11	31-62	17
12	Long Eaton Rangers	22	4	2	16	35-73	10

Sunderland Albion awarded 2 points when Birmingham St. George's refused to replay a match.

The only time a home International Championship game was played outside the two competing countries was at Shrewsbury in 1890, when a Wales v Ireland game took place.

In 1890 the Football League increased the minimum adult male admission price to 6d., maybe an attempt to limit the number of poorer and perhaps 'rowdier' supporters. In comparison to the costs of other popular, public leisure activities, football was quite expensive. Initially women were given free entry, but clubs were soon unhappy by the loss of revenue at the gate.

Yeovil Town were founded in 1890 as Yeovil F.C. and shared a ground for many years with the town's rugby club. In 1895, they became Yeovil Casuals and moved to play at the Pen Mill Athletic Ground. The club became Yeovil Town in 1907 but after joining with Petters United, the name changed to Yeovil and Petters United. Yeovil became the greatest F. A. Cup 'giant-killing' non-League team whilst playing in the Southern

League. Having won the Conference in 2002-03 by a record 17 points, Yeovil joined Division II.

Bournemouth was originally known from 1890 as Boscombe St. John's F.C., but in 1899 a number of enthusiasts secured local support and a meeting was held at a house in Gladstone Road - the new club started out as Boscombe F.C. In the early days Charlie Stevenson was responsible for many successes when the ground was at Castlemain Road, Pokesdown. In 1913-14 the club competed in the F. A. Cup for the first time and the following season became professional and entered the South Eastern League. In 1923 they joined the League and changed the name to Bournemouth and Boscombe Athletic.

In June 1890, a meeting was held in Manchester to form a league for good quality clubs in Cheshire and surrounding counties. The league was to be called The Football Combination and twelve clubs were elected. Stafford County resigned, while Derby St.Luke's and Witton (Blackburn) were unable to complete their fixtures - leaving just nine clubs finishing season 1890-91:-

		P	W	D	L	G	P
1	Gorton Villa	16	10	2	4	47-26	22
2	Macclesfield	16	9	3	4	44-27	21
3	Chester	16	8	4	4	42-30	20
4	Burton Swifts	16	9	0	5	55-28	18
5	Denton	16	8	1	7	39-32	17
6	Northwich Victoria	16	5	7	4	28-30	17
7	Hyde	16	3	4	7	25-39	10
8	Wrexham*	16	4	4	8	25-47	10
9	Leek	16	1	1	14	18-60	3

*2 points deducted

The first ever Football League representative team was in a match v the Football Alliance at Sheffield in the spring of 1891. The game was a 1-1 draw.

In season 1890-91, Derby County became the first club to fail to gain a single away point - other clubs with this same problem: Northwich Victoria 1893-94, Crewe Alexandra 1894-95, Loughborough Town 1899-1900, Doncaster Rovers 1904-05 and Nelson 1930-31.

In 1891 the umpires, who had been an unsatisfactory feature of the game and sometimes an obstruction to the referee, were changed in favour of linesmen. The main job for the linesmen was simply deciding when the ball had gone into touch or over the goal-line. The big step forward was that the referee, for the first time, had the power alone to decide on all issues and moved from his previous position on the touchline onto the pitch - the opinions of the linesmen being made subject to his

decision. The demand for referees led to the Referees Association being formed in March 1893.

For the 1891-92 season the penalty kick was introduced, following a proposal by Mr. J. Reed, Secretary of the Irish F. A. It was bitterly opposed by some amateurs, who argued that the new law assumed that footballers could be capable of cheating! When the penalty was first introduced, the lines should be marked:

1. 6 yards from the goal beyond which distance the goalkeeper should not advance.
2. 12 yards from the goal on which the player, standing alone, should take the penalty-kick, from which a goal might be scored.
3. 18 yards from the goal behind which all the players, except the kicker and the defending goalkeeper, had to stand until the kick was taken.

The main opposition to professionalism came from the South. Arsenal became the first club to turn professional as late as 1891, soon followed by Millwall and Southampton. The premier football competitions were therefore dominated by clubs from the North and Midlands.

Following the legislation of professionalism in 1885, there was still no stipulation as to the maximum or minimum wages. One of the greatest players of this period, Steve Bloomer of Derby County, was paid 7s. 6d. per week, but Sunderland were paying their players 30s. a week. At Fulham, the wage was 10s. and they were given an 'outside' job.

The first move to regulate payment to players concerned the signing-on fee in 1891. The Football League ruled it should not exceed £10.

Watford's history goes back to the late 1880s, when a team called Hertfordshire Rangers played in a meadow off Langley Road and R.C. Barker was a goalkeeper who was to earn international fame playing against Scotland. The team played in the Metropolitan section of the Southern League and won the County Cup in seasons 1888-89 and 1890-91.

In 1891 Hertfordshire Rangers amalgamated with Watford Rangers and the basis of the present club Watford came into being. They were admitted to Southern League Division II in 1896 and became professional the following season, winning that championship in 1899-1900. The chairman of Watford Urban District Council, Mr. R.A. Thorpe, saved the club. With financial support and the skill of player-manager, John Goodall, they were re-admitted to the League and opened a new ground at Cassio Road which was larger, with better facilities than Lords. Watford joined League Division III in 1920-21.

Small Heath were the first team to sell their ground rights, for a 2nd Round F. A. Cup game v Sheffield Wednesday in 1891-92 - the Yorkshire club paid £200 and won 2-0.

The first inter-League match with Scotland was played in 1891-92 at Bolton, ending in a 2-2 draw. The Scottish League being founded in 1891 and Irish League a year earlier.

Goal nets were invented and patented by J.A. Brodie of Liverpool in 1890. The first important match where nets were used, was North v South in January 1891 at Nottingham and for the first Cup Final at the Oval this year, becoming compulsory in 1892.

Rule changes made in 1892 were that the penalty kicker must not play the ball twice, and extra time was allowed for the penalty kick.

Football crowds then, as now, could be frightening and intimidating to a person who was not part of it. An unpleasant feature, which started in the 1880s, was referee-baiting - an article which appeared in *The New Football Mania* in October 1892 re a match in Shropshire read:-

> 'The referee we are told, was hooted and cursed every time he gave a decision and one of the spectators went as far as to threaten to throw him into a pond. Immediately after the match he was snowballed, in addition to which mud was thrown at him and he had to seek protection from the violence of the spectators.

> He took refuge in the pavilion for some time, but when he went towards the public house where the teams dressed, he found that there was a large crowd waiting for him and he was again roughly handled, his hat being knocked off and he received a blow on the back of the neck.'

Sheffield United created a League record away win in December 1892, when they won 10-0 at Burslem Port Vale in Division II.

The 1892 Cup Final was the last to be played at Kennington Oval (see photo), West Bromwich Albion defeating Aston Villa 3-0 before a crowd of 25,000. The crowds following the Cup were growing every year and the committee of Surrey Cricket Club, worried about their world famous pitch, refused permission for it to be used again as a football ground. The competition had attracted 163 clubs. Within the past ten years, the entries had almost doubled.

The F. A. considered every ground in the London area, but could not find one large enough - eventually the Manchester Athletic Club ground at Fallowfield was chosen for the final of 1893. The Athletic Club previously were housed at Old Trafford, but due to the new railway to the recently completed Manchester Ship Canal, had moved to Fallowfield in 1891.

A crowd of 45,000 paid for admission with many more left outside. The palisades (wooden fences) were not strong enough and by kick-off the crowd had overflowed along the touch-lines and the reserved seats invaded! It was only with many problems the game was completed - Wolves beat Everton 1-0 (see photo).

Despite the chaos of this Final, another important match was played at Fallowfield the following year - the Semi-Final for Bolton Wanderers defeating Sheffield Wednesday 2-1.

Liverpool were founded in 1892 by J. McKenna. Had Everton and their landlord not agreed to the amount of rent to be paid for the Anfield Road ground, the Liverpool club would not have been formed - the result was Everton moving to Goodison Park. A minority of players stayed at Anfield Road and formed a new club, Liverpool F.C.

At the start, the support for Liverpool was poor, but thanks to a £500 loan/gift made by the landlord Alderman Houlding, the club was in a sound financial position. The first season was a success as they won the championship of the Lancashire League, with a goal

F.A. Cup stolen in 1895 - never to be seen again!

average of 66-19, and the Liverpool Cup, without conceding a goal. Winning the cup proved a costly affair, as it was stolen and had to be replaced at a cost of £127!

Liverpool's immediate fame led to them being elected into the League II for 1893-94 and winning the Division at the first attempt. In 1900-01 Liverpool were crowned League Champions for the first time, dropping again into the Second Division, finishing top in 1904-05 and the following season becoming League Champions again.

The Football League was intended from the start to be split into two Divisions, each to consist of twelve clubs. Season 1891-92 had seen the League extend by two clubs to fourteen, with Stoke City returning and Darwen elected. It was not until the fifth season of the League that Division II got under way in 1892-93. Newton Heath, Notts Forest and The Wednesday were elected to Division I. Darwen, who finished bottom, were relegated to Division II - the first ever club relegated . Division I now had 16 clubs, but Division II initially had 12 teams - the first season of the Second Division ended:-

		P	W	D	L	G	P
1	Small Heath	22	17	2	3	90-35	36
2	Sheffield United	22	16	3	3	62-19	35
3	Darwen	22	14	2	6	60-36	30
4	Grimsby Town	22	11	1	10	42-41	23
5	Ardwick	22	9	3	10	45-40	21
6	Burton United	22	9	2	11	47-47	20
7	Northwich Victoria	22	9	2	11	42-58	20
8	Bootle	22	8	3	11	49-63	19
9	Lincoln City	22	7	3	12	45-51	17
10	Crewe Alexandra	22	6	3	13	42-69	15
11	Burslem Port Vale	22	6	3	13	30-57	15
12	Walsall Town	22	5	3	14	37-75	13

Bootle were not re-elected, Accrington resigned from Division I, but Division II was extended to 15 clubs by adding Royal Arsenal, Liverpool, Middlesbrough Ironopolis, Newcastle West End and Rotherham Town.

There was no automatic promotion and relegation at first. The Test Match system was used - the bottom three clubs in Division I met the top three clubs in Division II. Only three matches were played; one Division I team met one Division II club. The winners either retained First Division status or gained promotion accordingly.

The Scottish F. A. was formed back in 1873, but there was a long fight by the amateur element to keep the professionalism out of football. The battle finally ended in 1893, when paying players was made legal - in the

first year, fifty clubs registered a total of 560 players.

Gillingham started out in 1893 at a meeting in the 'Napier Arms', Brompton, due to the efforts of Alderman J. Barnes as New Brompton. Earlier there was a junior club New Brompton Excelsior. A company was formed and they were admitted to Division II of the Southern League in 1894, the other select members being Sheppy, Old St. Stephen, Uxbridge, Bromley, Chesham and Maidenhead. The ground which is now Priestfield Stadium, was bought and developed.

Most of the smaller clubs in this League struggled financially, but New Brompton faired better than some teams in Division I and later won the championship - a remarkable achievement as clubs like Tottenham and Southampton were in the League at the time.

In 1899 they met Woolwich Arsenal five times in an F. A. Cup qualifying game, before finally being victorious. New Brompton changed their name to Gillingham in 1913.

The players' wages problem came to a head in 1893, when the Football League proposed that footballers should be limited to £140 per year, including a maximum of £1 a week in the summer. This proposal did not receive the necessary majority and the idea of limiting wages was shelved.

The first attempt to form a Players' Union came in October 1893, when Wolves goalkeeper W.C. Rose sent a letter to all Division I club captains, proposing the formation of a Union 'to protect professional interests' - a Union was formed a few years later but it soon folded.

The amateur game was given a new lease of life for 1893-94 with the introduction of the F. A. Amateur Cup. Sheffield F.C. wrote a letter to the F. A. in August 1892, offering to put up a golden cup for competition among amateurs - the F. A., wanting to keep their position of authority, tactfully declined and instigated their own trophy!

The first Cup was won by Old Carthusians v the Casuals. The following year the winning club was Middlesbrough - the only future Football League team to have lifted the Amateur Cup.

Following the problems at Fallowfield, the Cup was moved to the new Goodison Park - a smaller crowd than expected of 37,000 saw a Division II side win the Cup for the first time, Notts County 4 Bolton Wanderers 1.

Bristol City's start was at a meeting on April 12th 1894 at the house of Mr. F.W. Kennan, within a mile of

Opening of Roker Park Sunderland in 1898

By the Marquis of Londonderry; Back row: J. Peers (Linesman), J. Cook (Groundsman), G. Young (Linesman), J. Fox (Referee), C.F. De Pledge, W.T. Doxford, M.P., Jas. Henderson, Lord Londonderry, J.P. Henderson (Chairman), C. Christton, R.T. Murray, J.J. Bentley (President of Football League), S. Todd, G. Childs, S. Wilson; Middle row: W. Williams (Trainer), W. Raisbeck, M. Ferguson, R. McNeill, J.E. Doig, P. Bach, A. McAlister, H. Wilson (Captain), J. Brown, P. Boyle, T. Campbell (Secretary); Front row: J. Crawford, J. Leslie, H. Morgan, J. Chalmers, A. Saxton.

Ashton Gate - a decision was made to form Bristol South End A.F.C., there were 18 members present, in addition to the Chairman, and the sum of £6 8s 6d. was promised.

The first match ever played by South End was September 1st 1894 v Swindon Town. The admission fee was 3d., enclosure 3d. extra, no dogs admitted! The club changed to Bristol City, following a meeting at the Albert Hall, Bedminster, became a professional side and joined the Southern League in 1897-98 - Sam Hollis was appointed manager and given a cheque for £30 and told to do the best he could with it!

Bristol joined Division II in 1901-02 and were promoted to the First Division for 1905-06. In 1909 they were in the Cup Final, losing 1-0 to Manchester United.

The Southern League was formed at a meeting on January 12th 1894. Arsenal first suggested the idea in 1892 but the following year went into Division II. Millwall Athletic was the next club to favour such a League and it was through their enterprise that a meeting was held. Other clubs present were Ilford, Luton, Clapton, Scots Guards, Reading and Chatham. Extra clubs, Royal Ordnance and Swindon formed the First Division of the new League, in addition to the teams at the meeting. Scots Guards dropped out and were replaced by Southampton St. Mary. There was also a Second Division with seven clubs.

The first season of the Southern League First Division in 1894-95:-

		P	W	D	L	G	P
1	Millwall Athletic	16	12	4	0	68-19	28
2	Luton Town	16	9	4	3	36-22	22
3	Southampton St. Mary's	16	9	2	5	34-25	20
4	Ilford	16	6	3	7	26-40	15
5	Reading	16	6	2	8	33-38	14
6	Chatham	16	4	5	7	22-25	13
7	Royal Ordnance Factories	16	3	6	7	20-30	12
8	Clapton	16	5	1	10	22-38	11
9	Swindon Town	16	4	1	11	24-48	9

This new League was, for many years, the main competition outside the Football and Scottish Leagues, helping to spread professionalism to clubs in the London and Home Counties area. Good professional players were enticed away from the North and Midlands, to challenge the supremacy of the great teams who formed the Football League.

In 1894, the referee was given complete control of the game. It was no longer necessary for players to appeal to him for a decision. The goalkeeper could only be charged when playing the ball or obstructing an opponent.

After two F. A. Finals in the North, the F. A. were determined to bring the match back to London. Crystal Palace had become a famous holiday centre. Nearby was its playing enclosure, formed in a natural bowl, with huge grassy slopes on the eastern side. This was capable of housing the many thousands of fans - this would be the venue for the next twenty years.

Only Time Cup Won Outside of England

F.C. Keenor, Captain of Cardiff City holding Cup with team-mates in dressing room after 1-0 victory v Arsenal in 1927

A crowd of 42,560 were at the first Final at Crystal Palace in 1895. Many never saw the winning goal, scored after only 30 seconds, when Aston Villa beat West Brom 1-0.

West Ham United developed from the Thames Iron Works team which had started in 1895, becoming West Ham United on July 5th 1900 after Mr. A.F. Hills of the Iron Works decided he would no longer run the works' club. The club immediately joined the Southern League and the first three seasons they were playing at the Memorial Recreation Grounds, Canning Town. Due to support being so bad, in April 1904, a move was made to the Boleyn Ground at Upton Park.

The club stayed in the Southern League until 1915 and after World War I, the club was elected to Division II in 1919. West Ham finished 7th, 5th, and 4th before runners-up, and promoted to the First Division for 1923-24. This was a successful period for West Ham, as they made their first appearance in the Cup Final of 1923 - although losing 2-0 to Bolton Wanderers.

The Test Match idea was changed for 1895-96 season, when the bottom two Division I teams played each of the top two Division II clubs twice - promotion and relegation was decided on the points gained by each team from its four games.

New rules introduced in 1895 were that Goalposts and Crossbars must not exceed 5ins. in width. Also a player taking a throw-in must stand on the touch-line with no run-up.

Association Football progress was slow in parts of Yorkshire, due to the vast number of Rugby clubs. One of the first steps was the start of the West Riding League in 1895 - its title disguised the fact it covered mainly mining towns south-east of Leeds. A few Rugby clubs of the Northern Union, Batley, Bradford, Halifax, Huddersfield and Leeds formed soccer sections - most were short-lived and poorly supported.

During the night of September 11th 1895, the F. A. Cup was stolen from the shop window of William Shillcock (see photo), a football and boot manufacturer in Birmingham. Aston Villa had given the Cup to Shillcock & Co. in Newton Row for exhibiting to the general public. A reward of £10, quite a large amount then, failed to produce any result and that original Cup was never seen again! It is believed to have been melted down to be made into counterfeit coins.

When Aston Villa received the Cup from the F. A., they were required to give a guarantee of the value of £200 and insured for that figure when lending the trophy to the shop - no amount of money would replace such a treasured piece of history. A new gold Cup was made

Terracing Collapsed at Scotland v England Match

In 1902, 25 people were killed at Ibrox Park, Glasgow.

by Vaughtons Ltd. copied from a 10 inch model given to each player when Wolves won the Cup in 1893 at a cost of £25. Aston Villa were fined this amount by the F. A.

Sheffield Wednesday defeated Wolves 2-1 to receive the new Cup in 1896. The winning goal was hit with such power that the Wolves goalkeeper Tennant was still wondering where the shot had gone. Seeing the ball lying in front of him, he kicked it up field thinking it was still in play. Tennant did not notice the kick-off and, after the final whistle, said to the Wednesday captain,

> 'When do we replay?' 'There's no replay, old man!' our captain remarked; 'We won by two goals to one, as you will see when we take the medals!' 'You can't have,' said the astonished goalkeeper, 'for only one shot passed me!'

The lightest player ever to appear in the League is believed to have been W. Hepworth, a Barnsley inside-right of the 1890s, who weighed around 7st. 5lb.

In 1896 the law for the markings of the pitch for the penalty kick was set out: (a) that the 6 yards line (for goalkeepers) should be a semi-circle of 6 yards from each goal post (b) that the 12 yards line (the penalty line) must run the whole width of the ground (c) that no 18 yards mark was necessary.

Between 1880 and 1896, the methods used by the forward line and the work assigned to half-backs changed to something like the system we see today. In the 1860s and early 1870s the forwards monopolised the attack and much depended on individual skill. A forward who could dribble well and trick his opponents was looked upon as a brilliant exponent - passing then was a little practised art.

Gradually the 'solo' forward game gave way to more combination of players in attack. Dribbling was still considered the chief asset among forwards, but these men realised that passing could be used as an extra weapon in attack.

Between 1896-1900, the passing game was developed further. So scientific had it become that critics thought this method of playing was being overdone. The problem being that the passing fashion tended to cramp the individual style and prevent players from using tactics which would make them 'stand out'. Events proved that passing need not interfere with individual skills - there were many players who became 'stars' before their careers were ended.

Loughborough Town turned up for a Division II game at Newton Heath in 1896, having lost their kit. In heavy rain they played in their clothes and had to travel home in the same outfits!

In March 1896, England beat Wales by a record score of 9-1 at Cardiff - the highest score by a Welsh team v England came earlier in 1882, winning 5-3 at Wrexham.

The International Football League Board was set up in 1897, when the Football and Scottish Leagues met to draw up a code of rules regarding the rights of clubs to retain players. In particular, the recognition of these rights by each League, so that the 'poaching' of players from one League to the other could be prevented. This year saw the word 'intentional' introduced into the law on handling.

Northampton Town came into the football world in 1897, its founders being a group of young assistant schoolmasters, most of whom were connected with the Northampton and District Elementary School's Athletic Association - in those days a flourishing organisation catering for young footballers. These young men discussed the possibilities of a professional soccer club. Money was scarce, but in due course, financial backing was forthcoming and Northampton Town was born.

In their first season 1897-98, they were admitted to the Northampton League, but at the end of the season the new club was £65 in the red. 'The Cobblers' carried on and joined the Midland and later the Southern League. An exhibition match v Sheffield United was not a financial success. The attendance was good but quite a number of the fans were 'gate crashers' who watched the game for nothing! Northampton were Southern League Champions in 1908-09, joining the League in 1920.

The Cheshire League was founded in 1897 following a meeting at the 'Cock Inn', Northwich, with a Second Division added in 1899 - the League folded in 1902 due to so many clubs joining The Combination. The first attempt at a Cheshire League had been made in 1890, but with only six clubs prepared to take part, it never got under way.

The only club to win both the F. A. and Amateur Cups was the Old Carthusians - defeating the Old Etonians to win the F. A. Cup in 1881 and the Amateur Cup in 1894 v Casuals and in 1897 v Stockton.

Portsmouth came into football at a time when the city wanted a team to take the place of the Royal Artillery (Portsmouth) Football Club who played in the Southern League. An F. A. Commission found the Artillery club had forfeited its amateur status by taking its players for a week's special training before an Amateur Cup match.

Two local sportsmen, G.L. Oliver, the headmaster of 'Olivers', a well known school and W. Wigginton, a builder and contractor and ex-Warrant Officer of the Royal Engineers, called a meeting to consider the formation of a professional club. Seventy attended and in a few weeks £4,950 was raised for the purchase of

Fratton Park. A company with a capital of £8,000 was formed by Sir John Brickwood, a Portsmouth brewer. Players signed up and in September 1899 Portsmouth played its first game in the Southern League at Chatham - Portsmouth went through just over two seasons without a home defeat.

Brighton and Hove Albion had an origin from Brighton United, a club formed in 1898 that died in its second season. Mr. John Jackson started the Brighton and Hove Rangers which was elected into the Southern League for 1901-02, but folded in June 1901. At a meeting at the 'Seven Stars' pub, Ship Street, a new third club Brighton and Hove United was formed - they took over Rangers' place in the Southern League and pitch at the County Ground. The name was changed to Brighton and Hove Albion because of objections by Hove F.C. The wage bill then amounted to £11 a week, which increased in 1903, when the club moved into Division I of the Southern League. The championship was won in 1909-10 and 1920-21, when Brighton joined League Division III.

Oldham Athletic started out in 1899. Earlier in 1895, John Garland, the landlord of the 'Featherstall and Junction Hotel' formed a club under the name Pine Villa. In 1899, the local professional club Oldham County folded - one of the liquidators persuaded Pine Villa to take over their ground at Sheepfoot Lane and change their name to Oldham Athletic. A good team of amateurs joined the Manchester Alliance and finished runners-up. The following season they moved up to the Manchester League and the Manchester Junior Cup was won in 1902-03.

The club continued to improve, being elected to the Lancashire Combination in 1904. In 1905-06 a limited company with a capitol of £2,000 was established, and arrangements were made to take over a lease of Boundary Park - the last season at Hudson Fold was 1905-06. Oldham joined League Division II in 1907, reached the Semi-Final of the F. A. Cup in 1913 and were runners-up in Division I in 1914-15.

Automatic promotion and relegation for the bottom two and top two teams of Divisions I and II was first introduced in 1898-99.

On November 26th 1898, a First Division game, Sheffield Wednesday v Aston Villa was abandoned because of bad light after 79 minutes play - Wednesday leading 3-1. The remaining 11 minutes were not played until March 13th 1899, during which time Sheffield scored another goal - final recorded result 4-1. Not surprisingly, a rule was brought in stating that a match must be replayed in full if not completed.

The first two brothers to play together for England as professionals were Frank and Frederick Forman of Nottingham Forest, three times in season 1898-99.

Season 1898-99 in the F. A. Cup, there were 235 clubs who entered - since the last Final at the Oval, 72 new clubs had joined the Cup battle. Very few of them had any real chance of winning, such as Hucknall St. Johns, Oswaldtwistle Rovers, Sandbach Ramblers, Long Eaton Rangers, to name a few. There was Preston's defeat of Reading 18-0, Bury's 12-0 v Stockton and Sunderland's 11-1 v Heathfield, but its these small clubs that make it the world's greatest football Cup Competition.

STEVE BLOOMER Derby County & England goal-scorer

Derby County's Steve Bloomer played his last Cup Final in 1899 v Sheffield United losing 4-1. Sheffield had four matches with Liverpool in the Semi-Final before winning. Steve Bloomer was one of the best goal scorers of all time, 352 goals in the League between 1892 and 1914 - a record later beaten by Dixie Dean. He had first learnt to play football with a schoolboys' club, the Derby Swifts, but quickly caught the eye of Derby. Scoring goals with either foot, he was the most dangerous inside-forward of his time - Steve Bloomer played his last match at the age of forty. (see photo)

In 1899 the F. A. made a suggestion to the Football League that there should be a transfer limit of £10 per player.

Cardiff City was originally formed in 1899, when they were known by the title of their ground - River Side. Like many clubs they started out as amateurs and grew to be the premier club in the Cardiff district, but experienced many problems due to Rugby being the main game played in South Wales. The team played next in the Old Park owned by the Marquis of Bute and then moved to Fir Gardens. In their amateur days, the club played on a public field known as Sophia Gardens.

The name of the club changed when Cardiff became a city and the present club was organised in 1910 and made the final trip to Ninian Park. Cardiff City are the only club to take the F. A. Cup out of England in 1927, defeating Arsenal 1-0 (see photo).

Scunthorpe United can trace their history back to 1899. Brumby Hall F.C. played at the Old Show Ground,

amalgamated with some other clubs and changed their name to Scunthorpe United. In 1910, the club merged with North Lindsey United to become Scunthorpe and Lindsey United. The team had to wait until 1926-27 for their first success, champions of the Midland League and again in 1938-39. The Lincolnshire Senior Cup was won in 1939 and 1940. One of the newer members of the Football League, Scunthorpe were not elected into Division III (North) until 1950, when the Division was extended to 24 clubs.

On tour in an F. A. team to Germany in 1899, the West Brom player Billy Bassett was man-marked by the same player everywhere on the pitch. To test the dedication of his German opponent, Bassettt strolled round the back of the goal - to his amusement his marker followed him all the way!

In the smaller towns, the behaviour of football fans was not always harmless, especially after the match. An example in 1899 gives us an idea of what must have been common at that time:-

> 'There were many thousands present at Shrewsbury on Easter Monday, and the combination of betting, drinking and bad language were fearful to contemplate, while the shouting and horse-play on the highway were a terror to peaceful residents passing homewards.'

By the turn of the century, most wing players took the ball up to the corner-flag before crossing into the goal-mouth, forwards moved five in a straight line, keeping the ball on the ground much more than today. Wing half-backs marked their opposing wingers but together with the centre-half, followed up closely behind the attacks of their own forwards; the full-backs covered the centre of the field, helping the centre-half to deal with the thrusts of the inside-forwards. That was the general tactic, which lasted until the late 1920s, when the change in the off-side law once again altered the whole attack and defence plan.

April 1900, saw the only time a goalkeeper scored direct from a goal-kick. Manchester City keeper, Charlie Williams, beat his opposite number J.E. Doig in the Sunderland goal, with the help of a strong wind, at Roker Park in a Division I match.

Swansea City started in a stronghold of Rugby, when in 1900 a number of ex-schoolboy players formed a club of their own and the Swansea and District League got under way - starting with ten clubs. As their first ground had no turf, only 'clinker', the players had to wear knee pads for protection! In 1912, the club were able to rent the Vetch Field from the local gas company and many improvements were made to the ground in 1913. It was a result of efforts made in 1912, that the present club was formed - the first match was v neighbours Cardiff City and Swansea won the Welsh Cup.

The club joined the new Division III in 1920-21 and reached the Semi-Final of the F. A. Cup in 1926, losing 3-0 v Bolton Wanderers at Tottenham.

Rochdale were formed in 1900, known then as Rochdale Town, and became members of the Lancashire League. A limited company was established in July 1910 when the title was registered as the Rochdale A.F.C. Limited. Since then, they have played in the Midland and Central Leagues before joining Division III (North) in 1921.

Football history was made in 1933 v Sutton Town in a Cup match. The scores were level with only seconds left, Rochdale were attacking and the centre forward, standing only three yards from goal kicked the ball into the net, at the same time as the whistle blew for time. The referee refused to allow the goal, on the grounds that the time expired while the ball was in flight!

Burnley goalkeeper Jack Hillman was not very successful in his attempt to bribe Notts Forest to lose a crucial match in 1900 - Forest won 4-0, Burnley were relegated and Hillman was banned for a year!

The first maximum wage rule came into force in 1901, when the limit was fixed at £4 per week - nine years later the amount was raised to £5, providing the increase was given in two rises of 10s. after two and four years service. At the same meeting, it also outlawed match bonuses - as partial compensation, players were awarded a benefit after five years, in case of accident or forced retirement, due to injury.

1901 saw another change to pitch markings (see photo): 'A suitable mark shall be made opposite each goal post, 18 yards from the goal line, behind which all the players except the penalty-kicker and the goalkeeper must stand'.

The following year, there was a big change to the penalty area markings - all the old lines were scrapped and we see the arrival of the goal-area, the penalty-area and the penalty-spot, as they are today. It was thought then that the earlier penalty-area was too big, stretching the full width of the field 12 yards from each goal-line.

There was a major disaster on April 5th 1902 at Ibrox Park, Glasgow during an International Championship match v England - part of the west stand collapsed with 25 people killed and many injured. The game, which had been going for ten minutes, was, surprisingly, resumed after half an hour - the result a 1-1 draw. (see photo)

The Northern Union Rugby League was having organisational and financial problems, resulting in some clubs disbanding or changing codes. When Manningham Northern Union club abandoned rugby for soccer in 1903 to reform as **Bradford City**, the Football League were keen to encourage the game in rugby's heartlands, giving them immediate entry into Division II, even though a playing squad had not even been assembled! Bradford were the first professional club in the West Riding of Yorkshire and there was strong local support right from the start - they inherited the claret and amber colours from the rugby team. An International League match between England and Ireland was played at Valley Parade in their first season.

Bradford were Second Division Champions in 1907-08 and won the F. A. Cup in 1911, 1-0 v Newcastle United at Old Trafford (see photo) before a crowd of 58,000, after 0-0 at Crystal Palace. Having moved into Division I, £10,000 was spent on ground improvements and providing covered stands.

Carlisle United were the result of Carlisle Red Rose and Shaddongate United clubs merging in 1903. Other Lancashire clubs had suggested there should be a team called Carlisle to gain better gates and success. The club was admitted to the Second Division of the Lancashire Combination for 1905-06 and won promotion the following season.

Due to the change in area for the Lancashire Combination, Carlisle were forced to play in the North-Eastern League - eventually winning the Championship making enough money to buy Brunton Park for £2,000. They did not join the League Division III (North) until 1928.

In the 1903-04 Cup there were major problems at Tottenham Hotspur v Aston Villa Round Two game - to get more fans in, extra seats were place inside the fence close to the touchline. At half-time with Villa 1-0 up, the holders of these seats invaded the pitch, followed by others onto the playing area, refusing to move despite being urged to do so by the officials - the match was abandoned. The crowd continued to cause trouble but the police prevented a riot taking place!

The F. A. Council held a meeting with officials from both clubs and ordered a replay at Villa Park. Spurs had to pay £350 from their share of the gate money, to be given to London charities.

In 1903, the F. A. passed a ruling that they control foreign tours undertaken by English clubs, letters arrived at the F. A. from Continental bodies asking about the control of matches between English and foreign clubs. It was suggested by the F. A. Secretary that a conference to be held in London early in 1904 to meet Continental Associations, but the foreign organisations made their own arrangements.

The only official international match played in mainland Europe before FIFA was formed was Belgium v France in Brussels on 1 May 1904.

In May 1904, the Federation Internationale de Football Association (FIFA) was founded in a little backroom in Paris. It was begun by representatives of five nations - France, Netherlands, Belgium, Switzerland and Denmark. From that humble start, it now has immense power and influence in global football affairs. It reflects the remarkable spread of the game, taken to various lands by the soldiers, sailors and emigrants from the British Isles.

In the F. A. Cup for 1904-05, it was decided that 5% of the gross gate money at all matches in the Competition Proper became payable to the F. A. - most of the money from the Semi and Final games now went to the clubs involved in these Cup ties.

Chelsea F.C. was born in a saloon bar of a small Fulham public house in the summer of 1904. Its founder was Mr. H.A. Mears, who became the owner of Stamford Bridge He had a meeting with some friends and confided his schemes to them - with such success that immediate negotiations were entered into for the promotion of a new club to be called Chelsea - this was after Fulham turned down an offer to buy Stamford Bridge.

A plan for the transformation of the ground was planned and a grandstand with seating for 5,000 was built, whilst the banks were extended and built up, capable of housing another 60,000 people. The task of signing a team was given to John Tait Robertson, a famous Scottish international who was playing for Glasgow Rangers, who was appointed manager. In less than four months Robertson had obtained a team for about £500, which included four internationals. For £50, Billy Foulkes was signed from Sheffield United and made captain - he was a much talked of player, six feet tall and weighed 22 stones!

Application to the Southern League was rejected but Chelsea were elected straight into the Second Division for 1905-06, promoted into Division I in 1907 and reached the Cup Final of 1915.

The English Schools Association was founded in 1904 and found a place on the council of the F. A., but it was not until 1927 that the F. A. fully identified itself with minor football by forming a standing committee to deal with this branch of the game. The F. A. was slow to appreciate its responsibilities, resulting in public schools, so important in the early days, turning to the Rugby code of football.

Leeds United evolved from the Leeds City club, started in 1904 from the original idea of old Hunslet players and supporters to form a club worthy of the city. Norman H. Hepworth, one of the oldest and most respected sportsmen in Leeds, gave his help and advice which was invaluable during the infancy of the club. The club put out an experimental team in 1904-05 and became tenants of the Holbeck's ground, when that Northern Union club was disbanded.

Leeds City were elected into League Division II for 1905-06. The club was not only expelled from the League in 1919 but also disbanded and their players auctioned off for making illegal payments to guest players during World War I. The manager, Herbert Chapman, chose to burn the club's books rather than submit them for inspection! The informer was the team's former full-back, upset at not being offered a better contract! Leeds reorganised the following year under its present name Leeds United and re-admitted to the Second Division in 1920.

Hull City were started in 1904 by three young men with more ambition than money, encouraged by the support given to minor Association football in a centre regarded as one of the hot-beds of professional Rugby. This bold trio entered into signing professional players, rented a ground and arranged an attractive programme of friendly matches with First and Second Division and other clubs for 1904-05 and decided to float a limited liability company.

It was agreed with Hull Rugby League Club to rent their excellent ground for three years, to play there when the Rugby team were not at home. Before the first season was over the Rugby League stepped in and would not allow any club under its governing body to benefit by any Association tenancy. Fortunately the Hull Cricket Club's ground within a quarter of a mile, was available and Hull City remained there until the 1930's. The Second Division was extended in 1905 when the club was elected. The Sheffield Wednesday full back, Ambrose Langley, was appointed player-manager.

The lowest number of points gained in one League season is 8 by Doncaster Rovers in 1904-05 - the club's record: won 3, drawn 2 and lost 29!

Within a period of seven years, Newcastle United reached the Cup Final five times, but, were unable to win one at Crystal Palace - the only victory was in a replay at Everton in 1910 - some compensation came with their League success in this period.

The first £1,000 transfer happened in 1905, when Alf Common was transferred from Sunderland to Middlesbrough - in 1902 he left Sheffield United to join Sunderland for £500. Common's transfer caused such a sensation that a special commission was set up to investigate - they were unable to report anything unlawful or underhand!

The attendances at matches rose continuously from the 1880s, with major increases from the late 1890s and again after 1906. In 1905-06 only Newcastle and Aston Villa had average gates of over 20,000 - by 1913-14, fifteen clubs had recorded that figure.

Crystal Palace started in 1905. The company that controlled the great building known as Crystal Palace proposed to start a professional team but the F. A. would not allow the company, who owned the ground on which the Cup Final was played, to join a league. A separate company was formed and became tenants of the ground. The Palace immediately joined the Southern League for 1906-7. There had been a football team of workers from Crystal Palace back as far as 1861.

From the Palace they moved to Herne Hill in 1915 and in 1919 played at The Nest before a final move to Selhurst Park, where they became Champions of the new Division III in 1920-21 season.

In season 1905-06, Bristol City won 14 consecutive League matches which created a new record, not equalled until the 1950s.

Norwich City were founded as professionals in March 1905, following a meeting in the Agricultural Hall and went straight into the Southern League for 1905-06, their opening game a 2-0 defeat at Plymouth. The original idea of a club was started by two local schoolmasters, who had a gathering at the Criterion Café in 1902. The first ground was at Newmarket Road and then in 1908 they moved to 'The Nest' in Rosary Road, Norwich. They caused a Cup shock in 1908-09, when Norwich went to Liverpool and won 3-2 before being knocked out by losing Finalists Bristol City. Like Crystal Palace, Norwich City were founder members of the Third Division in 1920.

In April 1906, the Scotland v England game at Hampden Park created a national debate following England's tactics to leave one defender back with the goalkeeper and push the other players within 20 yards of the Scots' goal line. In those days a player could be offside in his own half and there had to be three players between the attacker and the goal - the Scots crowd were not amused! The rules were then changed so that you could only be offside in your opponent's half - England lost the game 2-1.

Charlton Athletic were formed by a group of 14 and 15 year old youths on June 5th 1906, purely as an amateur organisation with no ambitions beyond local football. In their first season, the club finished top in the Lewisham League, the ground then being at Siemen's Meadow - that ground was not available for the second season and matches were played on Woolwich Common. Two years later, a ground was obtained at Pound Park, Charlton - with membership increased, a second team was run.

The first trophy won was the Woolwich Cup in 1909-10 and in 1913, the club was moved up a grade and a lease taken on an enclosed ground at Horn Lane, Charlton. Entrance was secured to the Senior Division of the Southern Suburban League and London League (First Division). They were Champions of the former League. In February 1920, Charlton turned professional and joined the Southern League, the South-Eastern and Kent Leagues and elected to Division III (South) for 1921-22. The Valley ground was vacated and moved to Catford. This was not a success and after a few months they returned to the Valley - originally a swamp with little prospect of it being turned into a football pitch!

Southend United started in 1906 - from 1890 there had been an amateur club called Southend Athletic which had played in the South-Eastern League but 1906 saw the team turn professional and change to their current name Southend United. This year the club joined the Southern League and finished top of the Second Division. The first ground as professionals was at Roots Hall, Prittlewell - after the First World War Southend moved to Kursaal until 1934, where the record crowd was 17,500 and moved to the Southend Stadium. The team became founder members of Division III in 1920.

Exeter City is another club founded in 1906. The first name of the club was St. Sidwell's Old Boys but turned professional in 1908, joined the Southern League and changed their name to Exeter City - Tottenham Hotspur had been elected into the Football League, creating a vacancy. Exeter were in this league until 1920, when they became founded members of League Division III. Clifford Bastin was transferred to Arsenal in 1930 for £2,000 and became an English international player.

Two of Exeter City's best seasons were in the 1930s. In 1930-31, they reached the quarter-finals of the F.A. Cup and created a record crowd of 20,984 v Sunderland. In 1932-33, Exeter finished runners-up in Division III (South) - League record goal-scorer F. Whitlow with 34 goals.

It was not until 1907 that the Football Players' and Trainers' Union was formed. The F. A. withdrew recognition of the Union in 1909 and gave the officials an ultimatum to resign or be forever banned from football! At the time of the ban, a strike of players was threatened - several did go without pay for 14 weeks before a conference was called in August 1909. The outcome of the meeting was that the players got their wages and the F. A. and the Union recognised each other. Since then, the Union has done much to improve the lot of the professional footballer, both as to wages and conditions of employment.

In 1907 there was a split in the amateur world. A section headed by a former Old Etonian and International player Hon. A. Lyttelton, broke away from the F. A. to form the Amateur Football Alliance. They started a Cup competition of their own, but little public interest was shown. This situation was healed after seven years, accepting that independence was no longer possible and some of the great schools moved back to the Association game.

The F. A. were building a basis for the future and schools were linked with League clubs: Charterhouse- Chelsea, Highgate-Arsenal, Malvern-Wolverhampton, Eton-Fulham, Winchester-Southampton, Westminster-Charlton, Forest-Tottenham, Repton-Derby County, Bradfield-Reading, Lancing-Portsmouth/Brighton, Brentwood-West Ham and Wellingborough-Northampton.

The annual F.A. Charity Shield was first played in April 1908 at Stamford Bridge, between the Champions of the League, Manchester United and winners of the Southern League, Queen's Park Rangers - United won 4-1 after a 1-1 draw. This was the formula for the next four years and then the F.A. chose the teams - usually Amateurs v Professionals or Cup holders v League Champions.

Huddersfield Town started out in 1908. For many years the town was a stronghold of Rugby and then Rugby League, but in 1897 a few followers of Association Football formed the Huddersfield and District League - after several attempts, this led to the beginning of a town club. The team first went into the North-Eastern League but, due to the travelling, this did not suit their needs. For the 1909-10 season Huddersfield changed to the Midland League.

Progress was quick, as in 1910-11, the club were elected into Division II and promoted to the First Division in 1920 under the control of a brilliant new manager, Herbert Chapman. Before that in 1919, the club nearly folded - the local newspaper headlined 'Town Club Dead' as £40,000 was owed to two backers and they even considered moving to Leeds. It was only through generous financial help from the Supporters' Committee that the club survived. The F. A. Cup was won in 1922 1-0 v Preston at Stamford Bridge.

On January 1st 1908 the F. A. wanted a maximum figure of £350 brought in for transfers, but after only four months, when discussed at the A.G.M., realised it was unworkable and so deleted this ruling.

Football was introduced for the first time at the Olympic Games held in London in 1908, United Kingdom winning the Final 2-0 v Denmark. Denmark had beaten France B 9-0 and France A 17-1. France refused to go for the third place play-off!

Hartlepool United were formed in 1908, but there was an amateur team going back to 1890 called West

Huddersfield Town in the 1920s

The Yorkshire club pictured on the left with the successful manager Herbert Chapman, who won the League with Huddersfield and later with Arsenal - Huddersfield were First Division Champions in 3 consecutive seasons and also won the Cup in the 1920s

Hartlepool which won the Amateur Cup in 1905. There were two very good Rugby teams in the town - Hartlepool Rovers and West Hartlepool, so there was some concern when the new association professional club came along. The United immediately joined the North-Eastern League, only dropping out for 1921-22.

During an air raid by a Zeppelin in 1917, the main stand, the pitch and fences were demolished - a claim of £2,500 was made - not a penny was received from the German Government! Hartlepools were original members of Division III (North) in 1921. One of the founders and first directors of the club, W.J. Coates (ex-Mayor) was still travelling with the team in the 1930s into his eighties!

England's first match v non-British opponents was on a tour of Central Europe in 1908. They first played Austria winning 6-1 and 11-1, Hungary 7-0 and Bohemia (now Czech Republic) 4-0 in Prague.

In December 1908, Sunderland won 9-1 away at Newcastle - scoring 8 goals in 28 minutes, the last 5 in 8 minutes. Newcastle had full-back Whitson off the field injured for the last 18 minutes.

A record number of three penalties saved in a League game was achieved by W. Scott for Grimsby Town v Burnley in February, 1909 - Burnley still won 2-0!

When Notts Forest defeated Leicester 12-0 in April 1909, a League inquiry established the Leicester players had been celebrating the wedding of a colleague!

The Scottish Cup was withheld in 1909 after the Hampden riot. Rangers and Celtic drew 2-2 in the first game and, after 90 minutes in the replay drew 1-1. There was no extra time scheduled but part of the crowd assumed there would be. When the players were leaving the pitch, the crowd realised there was no more play and destroyed the goalposts, broke down pay boxes and started a fire at the side of the pitch - police who tried to intervene were badly manhandled and stoned!

Fulham player George Parsonage was banned for life in 1909 for asking for a £50 signing-on fee from Chesterfield, the maximum fee allowed was £10. He later claimed the request was a joke!

Until now, goalkeepers usually wore similar shirts to the rest of the team but in 1909 it was ruled they must wear scarlet, royal blue or white to assist the referee - royal green was added in 1912.

Season 1909-10 saw the Second F. A. Cup fought over for the last time, when Newcastle defeated Barnsley 2-0 in the replay at Goodison Park after a 1-1 draw. The Council of the F. A. presented the trophy to Lord Kinnaird on completion of his 21 years as President. It had been discovered that the design, with no authority from the F. A., two seasons earlier, had been pirated in Manchester. The F. A. disapproved strongly, but the design of the Cup was not copyright.

Many designs were submitted from top silversmiths in the country for the third Cup, to match a budget of fifty guineas. The work was given to Messrs. Fattorini and Sons of Bradford. It weighed 175 ounces and was 19 inches high, including the plinth. On the ebony plinth was a large silver band on which were inscribed the names of all the previous winners.

Notts County sold their ground-rights to Bradford City for an F. A. Cup match in January 1910 for £1,000, Bradford won 4-2 - the takings fell short of the £1,000!

The Central League was formed in 1911 and initially comprised of 17 clubs, 20 in 1912 and 22 in 1919. It was regarded for many years as second only in importance to the Football League, consisting mainly of reserve teams from the top League clubs.

The longest period a player appeared as an amateur before turning professional with the same club, was ten seasons. R. Hawker achieved this with Luton Town, before signing professional forms for 1911-12.

In a game between Manchester City and Newcastle in January, 1912, the Manchester team managed to miss three penalties - the match ended 1-1.

The Cup Final of 1912 was 0-0 Barnsley v West Brom. The replay at Bramall Lane resulted in a 1-0 win for the Yorkshire side but not before extra time was played - for the first time in a Final. There was no rule for extra time in a first Final match, three times the game was not settled at Crystal Palace and the replay in the North - many fans were not amused about having to pay to see a second match! A meeting in July 1912, changed Rule 20 for an extra 30 minutes of play if scores were level after 90 minutes.

In 1912, a new law stated that the Goalkeeper was not allowed to handle the ball outside his own penalty area - previously he was permitted to do so anywhere within his own half.

The United Kingdom repeated their Olympic Games Final victory v Denmark in 1912, this time the score was a 4-2 win in Stockholm.

In 1913, opposing players were not to approach within 10 yards (instead of 6) of the ball, when a free-kick is being taken - the following year this also applied to corner kicks.

On January 11th 1913, the F. A. Cup was most affected by bad weather - of the 32 First Round ties, eight were postponed, eight abandoned and only 16 completed.

Several players have scored four goals on their League debut. The first player was F. Howard for Manchester City v Liverpool on January 18th 1913.

The first time a reigning monarch attended a Cup Final was in 1914 on April 25th, when King George V watched the last Final at Crystal Palace (see photo) when Burnley defeated Liverpool 1-0 before a crowd of 73,000.

By 1914, the footballers trade union claimed there were 4,740 professional players in England, located in 158 clubs. There were now few outstanding amateur players, so the professionals now formed the backbone of club and international football.

Burnley's goalkeeper, J. Dawson played a record 693 times for his club from 1906 to 1928 - due to injury, one of the few games he ever missed was sadly the Cup Final - reached only once during his career!

In 1915, Oldham player Billy Cook was banned for one year for refusing to leave the pitch when he was sent off in a game v Middlesbrough!

In April 1915, the F. A. permanently suspended 8 of the players who had taken part in a Division I game Manchester United v Liverpool. This was the outcome of an investigation which alleged the match had been 'fixed' for betting.

For the F. A. Cup of 1914-15, the Qualifying Competition was increased from 10 to 24 Divisions and brought a record entry of 476 clubs. Even though War had started, it was decided to continue with the Cup for one more season. Some of the rules were relaxed, so that war production was not disrupted. Replays were played on Saturdays with extra time where needed in all matches. There was one mid-week replay, Bradford City v Norwich City staged at Lincoln behind closed gates to avoid war production in nearby factories - it turned out to be a shambles as many people broke into the Sincil Bank Ground!

The F. A. changed the venue for the Final in 1915 to Old Trafford, before a crowd of 50,000, Sheffield United defeated Chelsea 3-0.

In February 1916, R.W. Benson, the Arsenal full-back left the field in a match v Reading and sadly died soon afterwards - he had not played for ten months and death was due to a burst blood vessel.

A Chelsea and Brighton goalkeeper T. Whiting, who played just before the War, could kick a ball from his goal-line over the bar of the goal at the other end - magical powers!

ALEC JAMES, Arsenal paid Preston £9,000 for him in 1929

MATT BUSBY, one of the Manchester City Cup-winning team in 1934

During World War I, the Football League carried on with two groups - Lancashire and the Midlands, with the exception of five clubs in the South who with the Southern League clubs played in the London Combination. A regional competition was also divided between a Principal Tournament in the first part of the season, followed by a Subsidiary one. For the record, the champions of the Principal competition: Lancashire Section 1915-16 Manchester City, Midland Notts Forest. 1916-17 Liverpool, Leeds City. 1917-18 Stoke City, Leeds City. 1918-19 Everton, Notts Forest.

In seasons 1917-18 and 1918-19, the winners of each section played each other home and away - the winner on the aggregate score being League Champions. The first season Leeds City defeated Stoke 2-1 on aggregate, followed in 1918-19 by Notts Forest 1-0 v Everton. The London Combination Champions were: 1915-16 Chelsea, 1916-17 West Ham United, 1917-18 Chelsea and 1918-19 Brentford. The F. A. made a rule that no payment or consideration to be made to a club or player for the player's services.

In Scotland during the War, Division I carried on as usual but the Scottish F. A. Cup was abandoned.

There had been an idea from the Football League clubs to persuade the F. A. to restart the Cup Competition in 1918-19, with various changes including no Qualifying Section and adding 20 clubs from the Southern League. The F. A. made the decision that the rights of all its members should be covered, so the scheme came to nothing.

The first League season after the War, 1919-20 saw both Divisions extended to 22 clubs - Glossop North End had resigned and the new clubs were: Coventry City, Gateshead, Rotherham County, Stoke City and West Ham United.

When the Cup began again after World War I, alterations to gate receipts meant that the income from the Semi and Final, after payment of expenses, was shared equally between the F. A. and the clubs taking part in these matches.

The Crystal Palace had been the venue for the Cup Final from 1895 to 1914, but had become a War Service Depot and was not yet available - eventually Stamford Bridge was chosen (see photo). Three Finals were played there: 1920 - Aston Villa 1 Huddersfield Town 0 after extra time. 1921 - Tottenham Hotspur 1 Wolverhampton Wanderers 0.

The 1922 Final was the first to be decided by a penalty, when Huddersfield defeated Preston 1-0 (see photo). The Preston goalkeeper, James Mitchell, an amateur who played in glasses and wore a blue and white bandana, danced about on the line and waved his arms trying to distract the penalty-taker Billy Smith! The F. A. were not impressed but did not change the law yet.

A previous Cheshire League had folded in 1902, but in 1919 the Cheshire County F. A. thought the time was right to form a professional League following a meeting at the 'Moseley Hotel' in Manchester. Some of the invited clubs were still tied to the Lancashire Combination, but in the end after many problems, the following teams started 1919-20 season in the new Cheshire County League: Altrincham, Chester, Crewe Alexandra Reserves, Dukinfield, Monk's Hall, Mossley, Nantwich, Northwich Victoria, Runcorn, South Liverpool, Tranmere Rovers Reserves, Whitchurch and Witton Albion.

The first time King George V watched a Football League game outside of London was in March 1920. He saw Manchester City v Liverpool at Hyde Road, Manchester.

Morecambe F.C. were formed on 7th May 1920 after a meeting at the 'West View Hotel' and joined the Lancashire Combination for 1920-21 season. Initially the club shared a ground with the Cricket Club with crowds of 3,000 for local derby games with Lancaster and Fleetwood. After one season Morecambe moved to Roseberry Park. A few years later after the purchase of the ground by President J.B. Christie, the ground's name was changed in his honour to Christie Park. They were Combination Champions in 1924-25 and won the Lancashire Junior Cup v Chorley before 30,000 spectators. The club's fortunes improved after the Second War with good F.A. Cup runs following - Morecambe were promoted to Division II in 2007.

A new rule brought in for 1920-21 season, stated that players cannot be offside at a throw-in.

Football was played more extensively by women after the First World War and a match at Goodison Park in 1920 attracted a crowd of 53,000 - raising £70,000 for charity, the Dick Kerr's Ladies v St. Helens. The 'stuffy' men of the F. A. stated that football was 'quite unsuitable for females', which meant they could no longer play at League grounds.

The creation of a Third Division had often been discussed in pre-war days, but it came about for 1920-21, thanks mainly to the input of a future League President, Charles E. Sutcliffe and the determination of a number of Southern League clubs. This new Division III was basically the First Division of the Southern League - Cardiff City had already been elected to Division II. To make up the number to 22 teams, Grimsby Town, who had failed to gain re-election to the Second Division, also joined as founder members. The first season of Division III ended:-

		P	W	D	L	G	P
1	Crystal Palace	42	24	11	7	70-34	59
2	Southampton	42	19	16	7	64-28	54
3	Queen's Park Rangers	42	22	9	11	61-32	53
4	Swindon Town	42	21	10	11	73-49	52
5	Swansea Town	42	18	15	9	56-45	51
6	Watford	42	20	8	14	59-44	48
7	Millwall	42	18	11	13	42-30	47
8	Merthyr Tydfil	42	15	15	12	60-49	45
9	Luton Town	42	16	12	14	61-56	44
10	Bristol Rovers	42	18	7	17	68-57	43
11	Plymouth Argyle	42	11	21	10	35-34	43
12	Portsmouth	42	12	15	15	46-48	39
13	Grimsby Town	42	15	9	18	49-59	39
14	Northampton Town	42	15	8	19	59-75	38
15	Newport County	42	14	9	19	43-64	37
16	Norwich City	42	10	16	16	44-53	36
17	Southend United	42	14	8	20	44-61	36
18	Brighton and Hove Albion	42	14	8	20	42-61	36
19	Exeter City	42	10	15	17	39-54	35
20	Reading	42	12	7	23	42-59	31
21	Brentford	42	9	12	21	42-67	30
22	Gillingham	42	8	12	22	34-74	28

Crystal Palace promoted to Division II and Grimsby Town transferred to new Division III (North), their places taken by Aberdare Athletic and Charlton Athletic.

In 1921, it was decided that goalkeepers in international matches must wear jerseys of deep yellow.

Wigan Athletic can trace their history back to 1921, when the club was formed as Wigan Borough and were founder members of Division III (North) the same year. There had been other clubs in Wigan from 1897, Wigan County, the first club to play at Springfield Park, Wigan United and Wigan Town but none of these teams lasted more than three years before folding. Wigan Borough resigned from the League in October 1931, due to financial problems but were Cheshire County League Champions in 1934-35 season. Having joined the Lancashire Combination, they were Champions of that league 1950-51, 1952-53 and 1953-54.

In June 1978, Wigan Athletic were voted into the League after an absence of 34 seasons, at the expense of Southport after tying 26 votes each - the second ballot saw them win by nine votes.

It was not planned for Division III to be filled by only Southern Clubs, the original proposal by Charles Sutcliffe had included a Northern Section, provided enough clubs of equal quality to the Southern Section could be established. In the end Division III (North) was founded for season 1921-22 but with only twenty clubs

taking part - including clubs which had previously been in the League like Grimsby, Lincoln City, Crewe Alexandra, Accrington Stanley, Walsall and Chesterfield. This is how the Northern Section's first season finished:-

		P	W	D	L	G	P
1	Stockport County	38	24	8	6	60-21	56
2	Darlington	38	22	6	10	81-37	50
3	Grimsby Town	38	21	8	9	72-47	50
4	Hartlepools United	38	17	8	13	52-39	42
5	Accrington Stanley	38	19	3	16	73-57	41
6	Crewe Alexandra	38	18	5	15	60-56	41
7	Stalybridge Celtic	38	18	5	15	62-63	41
8	Walsall	38	18	3	17	66-65	39
9	Southport	38	14	10	14	55-44	38
10	Ashington	38	17	4	17	59-66	38
11	Durham City	38	17	3	18	68-67	37
12	Wrexham	38	14	9	15	51-56	37
13	Chesterfield	38	16	3	19	48-67	35
14	Lincoln City	38	14	6	18	48-59	34
15	Barrow	38	14	5	19	42-54	33
16	Nelson	38	13	7	18	48-66	33
17	Wigan Borough	38	11	9	18	46-72	31
18	Tranmere Rovers	38	9	11	18	51-61	29
19	Halifax Town	38	10	9	19	56-76	29
20	Rochdale	38	11	4	23	52-77	26

Stockport County promoted to Division II.

Transfer fees as stated in the National Press are usually only estimated. In 1922 the Football League decided that all transfer fees should be treated as private and confidential.

Stamford Bridge was never planned as being more than a temporary venue for the F. A. Cup Finals - Crystal Palace came into the frame again, but was ruled out due to the huge cost of upgrading it to modern standards. There were plans for an Imperial Exhibition on a site at Wembley, so there was soon a suggestion that the F. A. should build a great stadium there.

Wembley Park was an undeveloped London suburb, a place for clean air, a few hills and trees - the park itself was a golf course, where it was planned to build a tower to rival the one in Paris, but this never got past the concrete foundations! In January 1922, King George VI cut a piece of turf to set things in motion. Within 300 working days, 250,000 tons of clay were removed and 25,000 tons of concrete brought in - slowly the huge amphitheatre took shape - total cost £750,000. A group of soldiers marched up and down the terraces to make sure it was safe for the general public!

On April 24th 1923, the last seat had been screwed into place four days before the first Final there - Bolton Wanderers 2 West Ham United 0 (see photo). A crowd of 126,047 passed through the turnstiles but there were estimates of another 50,000 who stormed over the barriers to get inside the ground. It was a miracle the match was under way forty minutes late, probably the only Cup Final not strictly played under F. A. rules as the fans in parts had spilled onto the playing area! The ground was originally known as the Empire Stadium.

Two players have scored an amazing 4 goals in 5 minutes. The first was J. McIntyre - Blackburn Rovers v Everton in 1922 and secondly W. Richardson - West Brom v West Ham in 1931.

The three Jack brothers played together with each of two League clubs. David, Donald and Robert were all with Plymouth Argyle in 1920 and then Bolton Wanderers in 1923 - a unique record.

In a Division III (North) match, Crewe Alexandra v Bradford in March 1924, there were 4 penalties awarded in only 5 minutes - a League record.

A League goal-scoring record for a goalkeeper was set in 1923-24 by A. Birch of Chesterfield - he scored five penalties in Division III (North).

In the last match of 1923-24, L. Davies missed a penalty for Cardiff City v Birmingham City. The result was 0-0. If Cardiff had won, they would have been League Champions - instead were runners-up on goal average and have never won the League!

Hereford United started in June 1924, after the amalgamation of St. Martins and RAOC, and played their first game on 30th August v Atherstone Town in the Birmingham Combination League. The first match in the F. A. Cup followed, losing 7-2 v neighbours Kidderminster Harriers. After four seasons they graduated to the Birmingham League and made their first appearance in Round One of the F. A. Cup in 1932-33 - losing 2-1 to Accrington Stanley. In 1939, Hereford became a limited company and joined the Southern League -finally going into League Division II in 2006.

In 1924, there was a change made to the corner kick - a goal could now be scored direct from the kick, following a proposal from the Scottish F.A. There was some confusion initially, as some players thought they could dribble the ball in from the flag - but the following season, the wording of the rule was changed.

Newcastle United were fined £750 by the League in May 1924 for playing weak teams in 7 matches prior to the F.A. Cup Final.

1925 saw the offside rule changed, also from an idea from the Scottish F. A. - a player could not be offside when two opponents instead of three were between

himself and the opposing goal-line. The old law had been in place since 1867, by the 1920s, full-backs had moved up almost to the halfway line and stoppages for off-side became monotonous. Now off sides became less frequent and many more goals were scored. In 1924-25, a total of 4,700 goals were scored in the League - under the new rule 6,373 goals - defensive re-organisation was inevitable!

The 7th February 1925 was a confusing day for Albert Pape. That day he travelled with Clapton Orient to play Manchester United. One hour before kick-off he was transferred to United and played against his old team and scored!

A Barrow forward F. Laycock was called off the field, in 1925 in a game v Rotherham, to sign forms for a transfer to Nelson F.C. - it was the last day of the season for transfers!

Manchester City missed a penalty v Newcastle United in the final match of season 1925-26 and were relegated from the First Division. The result was a 3-2 defeat for City - a draw would have saved them from relegation!

The first football match to be broadcast in England was First Division match Arsenal v Sheffield United at Highbury, January 1927 - the first Cup Final on the radio soon followed in April, Cardiff City v Arsenal. The F.A. banned the commentary of the 1929 Final, but the BBC succeeded in providing a service by setting up a broadcasting point near Wembley and engaged six reporters to leave the stadium in turn at 15 minute intervals to give a description of the game! There were various disputes between the BBC and the F.A. and Football League. It was 1937 before games were broadcast regularly.

Hughie Gallacher was rated as one of the best ever centre-forwards. He joined Newcastle United in 1926 for £5,500 from Scottish club Airdrie and became an idol on Tyneside. Although only 5' 6" tall, he was powerful in the air and he scored 36 goals in 38 games in 1926-27 - a club record. He played 23 times for Scotland, scoring 22 goals. (see photo)

HUGHIE GALLACHER of Newcastle United scored 36 goals in his first season, after a transfer from Airdrie for £5,500

Four brothers of the Keetley family all played for Doncaster Rovers. Joseph, Thomas and Harold were in the same team in 1926 - at the end of the season another brother Frank joined from Derby County.

When Stockport County player Hugh McLenahan was transferred to Manchester United in 1927, the fee was a freezer of ice cream - donated by United chairman Louis Rocca to County's bazaar committee!

The first amateur club to seek admission to the League was the Argonauts. Formed in 1928, they applied for membership of Division III (South) without success, as was the case in 1929 and 1930 - they had provisionally booked Wembley Stadium as their home ground!

In October 1928, the Newcastle United team which defeated Leeds United 3-2, contained 10 Scotsmen - only centre-half E. Wood was not Scottish-born.

The first defeat abroad of an English professional team was v Spain in Madrid in May 1929. An amateur England XI had lost 2-1 in Denmark in 1910.

A 1929 rule made a goalkeeper stand still on his goal-line when a penalty is being taken.

The youngest player to appear in the Football League was a A. Geldard for Bradford v Millwall in 1929, Division II - aged 15 years 156 days old.

A record for the oldest player to make his League debut was A. Cunningham, who was 38 years 2 days old when playing for Newcastle United v Leicester City in 1929.

Brentford broke a record in 1929-30 by winning all their 21 home games. Until now 5 other clubs had won all their home matches but with only a maximum of 18 home games played.

The referee of the Cup Semi-final Huddersfield Town v Sheffield Wednesday in March 1930, blew for time as a shot from Sheffield's J. Allen was entering the net. The ball had not crossed the line, so no goal was given - Huddersfield won 2-1.

The first World Cup took place in Uruguay in 1930. This country requested the opportunity of organising the competition. There had been a World Congress arranged by F.I.F.A. in 1928, when it was agreed to hold the Championship every four years. Only 13 countries entered, no England, and was won by the hosts Uruguay.

The first 12 games for Manchester United of season 1930-31 were all lost. One of the worst starts by any club in the League!

In 1931, the goalkeeper was allowed to carry the ball four steps instead of two. Instead of a free-kick for a foul throw-in, the throw now went to the other side.

Rochdale created a record in 1931-32 season by losing 13 consecutive home games. After defeating New Brighton 3-2 on 7th November, they lost all their remaining home matches. During this period Rochdale played 26 games, won none, lost 25 and drew one.

In season 1932-33, J. Ball, Sheffield Wednesday's centre-forward, converted a record number of 11 penalties in one season.

In 1933, Tottenham Hotspur proposed that players should be numbered. This proposal it was defeated at the AGM of the Football League - it was finally adopted in 1939, passed by 24 votes to 20.

Peterborough United reformed in 1934 and adopted the current name Peterborough United, previously called Peterborough and Fletton United after original clubs Peterborough City (Northamptonshire) and Fletton United (Huntingdonshire) merged. The new club played in the Midland Counties League until voted into Division IV in 1960 when Gateshead folded. The 'Posh', as they are known, won the League at the first attempt, scoring a Football League record of 134 goals!

In January, 1934 Stockport County created a record Football League score of 13-0 v Halifax Town. Against a powerful wind the half-time score was only 2-0, a further 11 goals followed after the break, 5 goals between the 50th and 59th minute - S. Milton the Halifax goalkeeper was making his League debut!

Arsenal full-back, E. Hapgood achieved the rare feat of heading a penalty v Liverpool in January 1935 -the goalkeeper Riley, fisted the ball back to Hapgood.

A goal-scoring record of ten goals in a match was achieved by J. Payne for Luton Town v Bristol Rovers in April 1936, Division III (South).

In 1936, players were no longer allowed to tap the ball into the goalkeeper's hands at a goal-kick.

Colchester United were formed in 1937 after the Colchester Town club was dissolved. The Town team dated back to 1867 and played at Layer Road from 1909, the ground originally owned by the Army until bought by the club in 1919. Colchester United immediately became a professional club and joined the Southern League and were Champions in 1938-39. They were not elected into Division III (South) until 1950 with Gillingham, when the Division was extended to 24 clubs.

Swansea Town's player W. Milne, a full-back, claims the unusual record of playing in 500 League games before he managed to score his first goal!

In 1937, players were not allowed anymore to tap ball into goal-keeper's hands when a free kick is taken inside the penalty area, weight of ball increased from 13-15 to 14-16 ounces and an arc of 10 yards radius from the penalty spot to be marked outside the penalty area.

Accrington Stanley, as we know the club today, were reformed in 1968 following a meeting at Bold Street Working Men's Club. The original Accrington F.C. were founded back in 1878, playing at Moorhead and became members of the Football League in 1888 - folding in 1896 after a 12-0 defeat to Darwen. In the meantime a club had started in the Stanley Street area called Stanley Villa in 1892, which became Accrington Stanley a year later. They resigned from the League's Fourth Division in 1962 due to financial problems.

In 1968 the new club bought their pitch, originally known as the Crown Ground, and joined the Lancashire Combination - a crowd of 620 saw the first match v Formby. In 1975, attempts were made to return to the previous Accrington Stanley's Peel Park, due to pitch problems, without success. The club joined the North West Counties League in 1982 and progressed via the Northern Premier and Unibond Leagues, before winning the Nationwide Conference and moving into League Division II in 2006.

Aldershot Town F.C. was born on April 22nd 1992, at the Royal Aldershot Officers Club at a public meeting - attended by 600 faithful 'Shots' fans. The club was accepted into the Diadora Isthmian League Division 3. A crowd of 1,493 watched the first game, a 4-2 victory v Clapton. An outstanding first season saw Aldershot champions by 18 points, remaining unbeaten at home - five divisions below the Football League but back in business!

The original Aldershot club was formed in 1927 and had joined Division lll (South) in 1932, but folded in 1992, due to financial problems. Aldershot Town won the Conference in 2008 and are in the League again.

Dagenham & Redbridge started as a club in 1992, when Dagenham merged with Redbridge Forest. In 1979, Ilford and Leytonstone joined and in 1988 they absorbed Walthamstow Avenue to become Redbridge Forest - Dagenham have a history going back to 1949. Redbridge moved in at Dagenham's Victoria Road Ground and were promoted to the Conference in 1991. Dagenham & Redbridge joined League Division II for the 2007-08 season as Conference Champions.

Milton Keynes Dons is the newest club, founded 21st June 2004 - nine months after Wimbledon moved to Milton Keynes and is legally a continuation of that team. Pete Winkelman, a music promoter and resident of the town wanted to build a stadium as part of a commercial development. Whilst there were four local non-League clubs in the borough, he felt it would be better to convince backers for an existing League club. He tried Barnet, Luton Town and Queens Park Rangers before he found Wimbledon who were looking for a new base. During the summer of 2003, the National Hockey Stadium was converted for use as a football ground. Mk Dons have returned the trophies and memorabilia of Wimbledon to the London Borough of Merton and make no claims on the history of the Southern club.

Back to the earlier football history, in the 1920s the four Divisions of the Football League were in place - the names have changed, as have promotion and relegation but there are still four Leagues. Wembley Stadium had been built and there were a few more rules of the game to be altered but modern football was now established.

One last thought, as it is now 145 years since the F.A. was founded, maybe sometime the offside rule will be finally sorted out!!

Index

Bibliography

'A HISTORY OF FOOTBALL' - Morris Marples (1954)

'SOCCER: THE WORLD GAME' - Geoffrey Green (1953)

'THE FOOTBALL ENCYCLOPAEDIA' - Frank Johnston (1934)

'THE OFFICIAL HISTORY OF THE F.A. CUP' - Geoffrey Green (1960)

'FOOTBALL AND THE ENGLISH' - Dave Russell (1997)

'HISTORY OF FOOTBALL' - UKTV History (2007)

'A PHOTOGRAPHIC HISTORY OF ENGLISH FOOTBALL' - Tim Hill (2005)

'THE ENCYCLOPAEDIA OF ASSOCIATION FOOTBALL' - Maurice Golesworthy (1957)

'ENGLISH LEAGUE FOOTBALL' - R.C. Churchill - (1961)

'MANCHESTER UNITED' - Percy M. Young (1960)

'ON THE BORDERLINE - THE OFFICIAL HISTORY OF CHESTER F.C.' - Chas Sumner (1997)

'IN RESERVE TRANMERE ROVERS IN THE CHESHIRE COUNTY LEAGUE 1919-1970' - Gilbert Upton (2000)

'THE FIRST NORTHWICH VICTORIA FOOTBALL CLUB 1874-1890' - Paul Lavell (1999)

HISTORY WEBSITE'S OF TRANMERE ROVERS, MACCLESFIELD TOWN, MANCHESTER CITY, HALLAM, SHEFFIELD, WIGAN ATHLETIC, YEOVIL TOWN, CHELTENHAM TOWN, MILTON KEYNES DONS, BARNET, COLCHESTER UNITED, DAGENHAM & REDBRIDGE, HEREFORD UNITED, MORECAMBE, PETERBOROUGH UNITED, WYCOMBE WANDERERS, ALDERSHOT TOWN (2008)

'THE FIRST NORTHWICH FOOTBALLERS' - Paul Lavell (2005)

'THE CHESHIRE COUNTY NEWS' (1883)

'100 YEARS OF SOCCER IN PICTURES' (1963)

'NON-LEAGUE FOOTBALL TABLES 1889-2007' - Michael Robinson (2007)

'FOOTBALL: THE FIRST HUNDRED YEARS' - Adrian Harvey (2005)

'THE TRIVIAL HISTORY OF FOOTBALL' - Past Times (2002)

'SHEFFIELD FOOTBALL CLUB - 150 YEARS OF FOOTBALL' - Steven Hutton, Graham Curry, Peter Goodman (2007)

'THE OFFICIAL ILLUSTRATED HISTORY OF MANCHESTER UNITED' - Alex Murphy (2006)

Acknowledgements & Thanks

I wish to thank the following for the use of their photographs:

COURTESY OF CHESHIRE MUSEUM SERVICE - Manchester United in 1909

ASSOCIATED SPORTING PRESS, 166 FLEET STREET, LONDON E.C.4

ROBERT HALE LTD., 45-47 CLERKWELL GREEN, LONDON

BLACKBURN WITH DARWEN LIBRARY & INFORMATION SERVICES - Blackburn Rovers 1884

SECKER & WARBURG, 7 JOHN STREET, BLOOMSBURY, LONDON

WILLIAM HEINEMANN LTD., LONDON

PHOENIX HOUSE LTD., 38 WILLIAM IV STREET, CHARING CROSS, LONDON W.C.2

PARAGON, QUEEN STREET HOUSE, 4 QUEEN STREET, BATH

HYNDBURN BOROUGH COUNCIL, ACCRINGTON - Accrington F.C. 1886

ORION PUBLISHING GROUP LTD., ORION HOUSE, 5 UPPER ST MARTIN'S LANE, LONDON

PETER HOLME, NATIONAL FOOTBALL MUSEUM, PRESTON - Uppingham, Oxford, Cambridge, Blackburn Olympic. Eton - Priory Collection at the National Football Museum

Sheffield F.C., Steve Hutton (HR Media) and historian Graham Curry

Paul Lavell, Northwich - re Davenham F.C.

John Steele, Hallam F.C. Historian

Pam Bann for her excellent proof reading skills